THE
HISTORY
of the
HOLOCAUST

THE
HISTORY
of the
HOLOCAUST

A
CHRONOLOGY
OF
QUOTATIONS

HOWARD J. LANGER

JASON ARONSON INC.
Northvale, New Jersey
Jerusalem

This book was set in 11pt. Cheltenham Book by Alabama Book Composition of Deatsville, Alabama, and printed and bound by Book-mart Press of North Bergen, New Jersey.

Copyright © 1997 by Howard J. Langer.

We gratefully acknowledge the courtesy of Pantheon Books, Inc., in granting permission to reprint material from *Shoah: An Oral History of the Holocaust*, by Claude Lanzmann, © 1985.

10 9 8 7 6 5 4 3 2 1

Library of Congress Cataloging-in-Publication Data

The history of the Holocaust: a chronology of quotations / compiled
   and edited by Howard J. Langer.
         p. cm.
   Includes bibliographical references and index.
   ISBN 0-7657-5956-X (alk. paper)
   1. Holocaust, Jewish (1939–1945)—Personal narratives.
   2. Antisemitism—Germany. I. Langer, Howard.
   D804.195.H57 1997
   940.53′18—dc20   96-33636

Manufactured in the United States of America. Jason Aronson Inc. offers books and cassettes. For information and catalog write to Jason Aronson Inc., 230 Livingston Street, Northvale, New Jersey 07647.

For Anne,
who put a human face
on six million
statistics.

If I am not for myself, who will be for me?
But if I am for only myself, what am I?
And if not now, when?

Hillel
1st Century B.C.E.

Contents

Acknowledgments

To begin with, I would like to acknowledge the loving assistance of my wife, Florence. It is a cliché to use the phrase, "without whose help this book would not have been possible. . . ." However, it is certainly justified here. She has not only been my chief researcher, but my driver, critic, cheerleader, and best friend.

I wish to thank the following for their courtesy and assistance: the staff of the New City (Rockland County, N.Y.) Public Library; the staff of the Finkelstein Memorial Library, Spring Valley, N.Y.; the staff of YIVO in New York City; the Holocaust Memorial Museum in Washington, D.C.; Dr. Ellen Frankel of the Jewish Publication Society; the Rev. Daniel F. Martensen of the Evangelical Lutheran Church in America; Jason Aronson, Arthur Kurzweil, Pamela Roth, and Steven Palmé.

I also want to thank all those friends and relatives who sent me books, cut out news articles, taped videos, and provided ideas and suggestions.

There were many publications used in compiling these quotations. Whenever possible, I have tried to cite the original source rather than a secondary one.

Every book listed in the bibliography was an important

one. Some, however, were extremely useful to me for different reasons, and I would like to give them special mention.

The best overall study of the Hitler era in Europe is the classic *The Rise and Fall of the Third Reich* by William L. Shirer. In his book, the Holocaust is depicted within the context of the Nazi rise to power and the war in Europe.

An extraordinary volume is *Hitler's Death Camps: The Sanity of Madness* by Konnilyn G. Feig. She takes the reader to every major concentration camp site, as it exists today, and gives its history, geography, and a map of what it looked like during the Holocaust. She does not spare the reader in describing what horrors occurred there. One thing more: she gives the reader directions on how to get there today, because many local residents—and some local travel guides—may stare blankly if asked about a camp's location.

The outstanding work on American policy during the war against European Jewry is *The Abandonment of the Jews: America and the Holocaust* by David Wyman. The book, thoroughly researched, is a devastating indictment.

Beyond Belief: The American Press and the Coming of the Holocaust, 1933–1945 by Deborah E. Lipstadt is an exhaustive study of the newspaper and magazine stories in America during the Hitler era. Included are not just the news stories, but evaluations of how and where the articles were placed in the newspapers.

Many books have been written on a single action or event of Jewish resistance. *They Fought Back,* edited and translated by Yuri Suhl, is a compilation of a number of such instances. Several of the accounts were prepared specifically for his anthology.

An excellent account of Crystal Night—not merely in terms of the pogroms but of the political consequences for Nazi Germany—is *Krystallnacht* by Anthony Read and David Fisher. It is both well-written and well-researched.

Finally, there is an extraordinary book about what it feels like to be German after the Holocaust. *What Did You Do in the War, Daddy?,* by Sabine Reichel, is a sensitive depiction of feelings of guilt and innocence among different German generations.

—H.J.L.

Introduction

Many years ago, science fiction writer Ray Bradbury wrote a short story called "A Sound of Thunder." It took place at a time in the future when all the wild animals were extinct. The only way to hunt was to go back in the past in a time machine. A hunter could choose any animal he wished to hunt as long as he did not step off the time machine. The idea was to prevent any change in the long-term environment and ecosystem. (The targeted animal, researchers had determined, was about to die anyway.)

In the story, the hunter stalks a dinosaur, but accidentally steps off the time machine. On his return home, he discovers that the world has changed. When he had stepped off the time machine, he had accidentally stepped on a beautiful butterfly.

One butterfly and the whole world changed.

And what can be said of the deaths of six million Jews during the Holocaust? Not one butterfly, but six million members of a group whose contributions to science, medicine, literature, music, the arts, philosophy, and religion have been so disproportionate to their numbers in the world.

Though this is a book of *Holocaust* quotations, it does not start at 1933 and end in 1945—the Nazi era. It goes back two millennia to the earliest anti-Jewish teachings, laws, and acts of violence. The quotations then go through the Nazi period, ending with the period of reflection following the Holocaust.

Throughout the book, I have tried to avoid an overemphasis on the descriptions of atrocity and murder. Those accounts are, after all, too well known. But what I was seeking were more subtle documents, such as laws and speeches, conferences and discussions, superstitions and religious beliefs tending to teach contempt of Jews and Judaism.

The aftermath of the Holocaust includes commentaries by leading scholars, material from the Nuremberg and Eichmann trials, and post-Holocaust statements by the Roman Catholic and Lutheran churches.

When reading the quotations of individuals, be sure to note the dates involved. Earlier quotations by Nazi victims may show a bitterness and rage that may have changed over time. Likewise, the statements of Nazi officials may also change even more dramatically from the time of Nazi power to the time of judgment.

Interspersed in the book are historical dates to keep the material in chronological context with what else was going on in the world at the time: Hitler becoming chancellor, the Nazi attack on Russia, Pearl Harbor, and so on.

Huge volumes have been written about specific aspects of the Holocaust, such as atrocities, diplomacy, medical experiments, war crimes trials, rescue attempts, ghettos, rescuers, and other aspects of the Holocaust. I recommend the bibliography for readers and researchers seeking greater depth. This book is an attempt to do no more than pull together quotations which illustrate the different aspects. In most cases, the quotations chosen are brief. In a few cases, they are longer. In those cases, I felt a single long quote would tell the story much better than many brief ones.

The "Who's Who" section offers a brief identification of those quoted in this book. Some of the biographical material will become dated, and suggested changes and corrections are welcomed for future editions.

The story of the Holocaust is a story of euphemisms—the Final Solution, resettlement to the East, special treatment. Those were Hitler's euphemisms. But the West had its euphemisms also.

One of the first meetings on Jewish refugees was the Evian conference of 1938. If you read the official statement on the conference (see pages 65–67), you may be puzzled to discover that nowhere in the document do the words *Jew* or *Jewish*, or even *refugee* appear. (The text has been trimmed down for space reasons, but those terms were never used.) Jewish refugees were called "involuntary emigrants."

One thing more. Various countries of the world are called upon to contribute to help these involuntary emigrants. And the country from which they come is asked to make its "contribution" by allowing these emigrants to leave with their own property!

Of all the quotations in this book, the Evian conference report is probably the most cynical, though you may find some cynical quotations of your own.

This was not an easy book to put together. The material was all there—but it was very, very heavy.

Before he died, a friend and colleague, Gideon Chagy, talked to me about doing a book on a world without any of the Jewish contributions. He never had a chance to write it. Perhaps the real story is many centuries away, when there are no descendants of the six million. What will that world be like?

—Howard J. Langer

PRELUDE

From the Gospel

Pilate said unto them, What shall I do then with Jesus which is called Christ? They all say unto him, Let him be crucified. . . . When Pilate saw that he could prevail nothing, but that rather tumult was made, he took water, and washed his hands before the multitude, saying, I am innocent of the blood of this just person: Then answered all the people, and said, His blood be on us, and on our children.

> The Gospel According to
> Matthew
> first century C.E.

Church Rules

Intermarriage or sexual intercourse between Christians and Jews is prohibited.

> Synod of Elvira
> 306

331 C.E.

The Emperor Constantine orders Jews to take part in the defense of the city of Cologne. This is the first historical reference to the presence of Jews in the Rhineland.

CHARACTERIZING JEWS

[The Jews are] murderers of the Lord, assassins of the prophets, rebels against God, God haters . . . advocates of the devil, race of vipers, slanderers, calumniators, dark-minded people, leaven of the Pharisees, cyanhydrin of demons, sinners, wicked men, stoners, and haters of righteousness.

> Saint Gregory of Nyssa
> *Homilies on the Resurrection*
> 4th Century

Cited in Anti-Semitism in Times of Crisis, *edited by Sander L. Gilman and Steven T. Katz.*

OFFICE BAN

Jews may not hold public office.

> Synod of Clermont
> 535

NO SERVANTS

Jews may not employ Christian servants or own Christian slaves.

> Third Synod of Orleans
> 538

Special Clothes

Christians must wear blue belts; Jews must wear yellow belts.

> Caliph Omar II
> Decree
> 634–44

No Jewish Doctors

Christians may not patronize Jewish doctors.

> Trulanic Synod
> 692

The Jew Oath

From the days of Charlemagne, a Jew appearing in a German court in a case where there were no witnesses had to swear a special oath to prove his veracity. Unlike the oaths administered to Christians, the *Judeneid* [Jew oath] was insulting and degrading. The Jew had to kneel before the judge on the skin of a pig and pronounce all sorts of curses that would befall him if he did not speak the truth.

> *Ashkenaz: The German
> Jewish Heritage*
> Edited by Gertrude Hirschler
> Events ca. 700

The Jew Oath in Germany lasted into the 19th century.

1095–1291 C.E.

Following an appeal by Pope Urban II, the Christian nations of Western Europe undertake military expeditions, which they call Crusades, to free the Holy Land from the Moslems. On their way to Palestine, the Crusaders rob or murder thousands of Jews throughout Europe. When the Crusades end, the Moslems are in complete control of the Holy Land.

Pope Innocent on the Jews

It was wrong to kill the Jews, for they must survive to remind the Christians of divine law, though they must live in shame as outcasts until they "seek the name of Jesus Christ the Lord."

Pope Innocent III
Early 13th century

Cited in Ideology of Death *by John Weiss.*

Hat and Badge

The "Jew hat," shaped like a cone or a funnel, and the yellow Jewish badge, shaped like a ring or a wheel, were officially mandated in Germany during the 13th century. Some historians claim that both the hat and the badge had already been noted in Germany a century earlier.

There were exact specifications for the yellow badge: it had to be two fingers' breadths wide and four fingers' breadths long, and it had to be worn on the outer garment.

The purpose of these identifying marks was to set the Jews apart from the non-Jews. All male Jews twelve years of age and older were obliged to wear them.

Ashkenaz: The German
Jewish Heritage
Edited by Gertrude Hirschler
Events of the 13th century

1286 C.E.

In Munich, Christians set fire to a synagogue, killing 186 Jews.

A DEATH IN NORWICH

In his [King Stephen's] time, the Jews of Norwich [England] bought a Christian child before Easter and tortured him with all the torture that our Lord was tortured with, and on Good Friday hanged him on a cross on account of our Lord, and then buried him. They expected it would be concealed, but our Lord made it plain that he was a holy martyr, and the monks took him and buried him with ceremony in the monastery, and through our Lord he works wonderful and varied miracles and he installed St. William.

> English tract
> 1155

Cited in The Blood Libel Legend: A Casebook in Anti-Semitic Folklore, *edited by Alan Dundes.*

THE JEWISH BADGE

Jewish clothing will be marked with a badge.

> Fourth Lateran Council
> Canon 68
> 1215

GHETTOS ESTABLISHED

Compulsory ghettos are established for Jews.

> Synod of Breslau
> 1267

TROUBLE IN SPAIN

Evil has befallen us . . . throughout the length and breadth of the provinces of Castile and in the Kingdom of Catalonia in the year 1391. . . . And for twenty-two years thereafter those who were left in Castile were a parable and a by-word, their situation becoming ever worse. . . . They were required to change their garments, and various trades and leasings and crafts were denied to them. . . . Those who had lived comfortably in their homes were expelled from palaces of ease and delight. . . . All Jews dwelt in shacks both in summer and winter in shame and misery . . . for they had not learnt crafts wherewith to make a living. . . . And so it happened in the Kingdom of Aragon to the remaining communities when a new king rose against them to enact new discriminations.

R. Solomon ibn Lahmish Alami
Iggeret Mussar
1415

Cited in History of the Jewish People, *edited by H. H. Ben-Sasson, 1976.*

PAPAL DECREE

We decree and order that from now on, and for all time, Christians shall not eat or drink with Jews, nor admit them to feasts, nor cohabit with them, nor bathe with them. Christians shall not allow Jews to hold civil honors over Christians, or to exercise public offices in the state.

Pope Eugenius IV
Decree
1442

1480–1825 C.E.

Between 30,000–100,000 Jews are burned to death by the Spanish and Portuguese Inquisitions at *auto-da-fe* (act of faith) ceremonies.

MARCH 31, 1492

Edict of Expulsion is announced, involving removal of the Jews from Spain.

Expulsion from Spain

In the year 1492 during the reign of Ferdinand, God again punished the remnant of the Jewish people, by having them expelled from Spain. Ferdinand had wrested the city of Granada from the Moslems on January 7 and soon thereafter ordered all Jews to be deported. . . . The king gave them three months' time to leave the country. . . . There was little time left and . . . they sold their homes, their land, and their cattle for paltry sums. . . . One hundred and twenty thousand persons left for Portugal, following an agreement between the king of Portugal. . . . The Jews had to pay one ducat for each person admitted and one quarter of their goods in order to stay six months.

> Contemporary account
> Spain
> Events of 1492

Cited in The Jew in the Medieval World *by Jacob R. Marcus, 1938.*

Martin Luther on the Jews

What shall we Christians do with this rejected and condemned people, the Jews? . . .

First, their synagogues should be set on fire, and whatever does not burn up should be covered or spread over with dirt so that no one may ever be able to see a cinder or stone of it. . . .

Second, . . . their houses also be razed and destroyed for they pursue in them the same aims as in their synagogues. . . .

Third, . . . all their prayer books and Talmudic writings . . . be taken from them.

Fourth, . . . their rabbis be forbidden to teach henceforth on pain of loss of life and limb. . . .

Fifth, . . . safe conduct of the highways be abolished completely for the Jews. . . .

Sixth, . . . that usury be prohibited to them, and that all cash and treasure of silver and gold be taken from them and put aside for . . . the following: Whenever a Jew is sincerely converted, he should be handed over one hundred, two hundred or three hundred florins. . . . With this he could set himself up in some occupation for the support of his poor wife and children and the maintenance of the old or feeble. . . .

Seventh, . . . [put] a flail, an ax, a hoe, a spade, a distaff or a spindle into the hands of young, strong Jews and Jewesses and letting them earn their bread in the sweat of their brow. . . .

> Martin Luther
> *On the Jews and Their Lies*
> 1543

ON JEWS AND MISERY

It is a marvelous thing to observe the Jewish people existing for so many years and always in misery, for it is necessary as proof of Jesus Christ both that they should continue to exist, and that they should be miserable because they crucified him.

> Blaise Pascal
> Mid-17th century

END OF AN ITALIAN GHETTO

For, praised be the Almighty, the French have entered the city with great speed, swifter than on the wings of eagles, and more powerful than lions. Immediately they inquired the where-abouts of the Jewish ghetto, and . . . entered the ghetto, and said to the Jews: "Jews, our brothers, fear no longer the wicked Christians who seek to harm you! We have come to save you, for God has shortened our journey so we might rescue you from the hands of these people!"

> An Italian Jew
> Ancona, Italy
> 1798

Cited in Jewish Survival in the World Today *by Abraham Duker, 1940.*

SCORNED ON BOTH SIDES

I am now hated by Christian and Jew alike. I much regret that I had myself baptized. I don't perceive that things have gone better for me. On the contrary, I have since had nothing but misfortune.

> Heinrich Heine
> Letter to Moses Moser
> 1825

Cited in The Jews of Germany *by Ruth Gay.*

SECOND THOUGHTS ON CONVERSION

Jew, Jew, that is the last red cent in the miserable bank of their wit. But after all this, I wish that I could have my three louis d'or back, those with which I honored the pastor for my Christianity. I have been baptized now for 18 years and it doesn't help me. Three louis d'or for a little place in the German madhouse. It was pure waste!

> Karl Ludwig Borne
> 1836

Cited in The Jews of Germany *by Ruth Gay.*

MARX ON THE JEWS

What is the worldly religion of the Jews? Money. That is the jealous God of Israel before whom no other God can maintain his place.

> Karl Marx
> Essay
> "On the Jewish Question"
> 1844

FROM A FRENCH ANTI-SEMITE'S NOTEBOOK

Demand their expulsion from France with the exception of individuals married to French women. Abolish the synagogues; don't admit them to any kind of employment; pursue finally the abolition of this cult. It is not for nothing that the Christians call them deicides. The Jew is the enemy of the human race. One must drive this race back to Asia or exterminate it. . . . By the fire or fusion, or by expulsion the Jew must disappear.

> Pierre-Joseph Proudhon
> 1847 notebook

BAKUNIN ON THE JEWS

[Jews are] an exploiting sect, a bloodsucking people, a unique devouring parasite, tightly and intimately organized.

Mikhail Bakunin
Mid-19th century

OCTOBER 15, 1864

In Brussels, a satire about the government of Napoleon III is published. It is called *Dialogues in Hell Between Montesquieu and Machiavelli*, by French lawyer Maurice Joly. The book will be suppressed in France, and its author sentenced to prison.

At the close of the 19th century, the book will be plagiarized and re-edited by the Czar's secret police. It will emerge in Western Europe in 1919 as *The Protocols of the Learned Elders of Zion,* a fabrication citing a Jewish plot to control the world.

Higher Education in Imperial Germany

The anti-Semitic pamphlets of the 1870s denounced the intellectual "domination" of Germany by Jews. In his anti-Semitic speeches Adolf Stocker, one of the fathers of modern political anti-Semitism, decried the "disproportionate onslaught on institutions of higher education" by Jews and "the Judaization of girls' grammar schools." By the end of the 1870s, more and more fraternities excluded Jews, some by statute and others by "selective reception." As anti-Semitism mushroomed, becoming a social norm on German campuses, the theme of "Jewish competition" cropped up. Particularly during the severe crisis in the academic labor market of the 1880s, students complained: [The Jews inhabit] our universities in vast numbers and so Jewish doctors push out Christians, Jewish mouths disproportionately emit jurisdiction and law."

> Marion A. Kaplan
> *The Making of the Jewish Middle Class*
> Citing events of the 1870s–1880s in Germany

A German Scholar on Jews

Jews [are] decayed parasites and usurious vermin.

> Paul de Lagarde
> Germany
> Late 19th century

Proudhon on the Jews

The Jew is by temperament an anti-producer, neither a farmer, nor an industrialist, nor even a true merchant. He is an intermediary, always fraudulent and parasitic, who operates in trade, as in philosophy, by means of falsification, counterfeiting, horse-trading. . . . It is the principle of evil, Satan . . . incarnated in the race of Shem.

> Pierre-Joseph Proudhon
> *Caesar and Christianity*
> 1883 (published after his death)

AN ENGLISHMAN VIEWS JEWS AND GERMANS

[The Germans] are menaced by a complete moral, intellectual, and material ruin if a strong reaction does not set in in time against the supremacy of the Jews, who feed upon [Germans] and suck out—at every grade of society—their very life blood.

> Houston Stewart Chamberlain
> Letter
> 1888

AN ASSESSMENT BY TOLSTOY

Anti-Semitism is . . . a pathological condition, a peculiar form of sexual perversion.

> Leo Tolstoy
> 1889

At the Dreyfus Court-Martial

The traitor, there he is! . . . I swear to it.

> Commandant Hubert Henry
> pointing to French Army
> Captain Alfred Dreyfus, a
> Jew charged with spying
> for Germany
> December 1894
> France

Mob Calls for Death

Death to the Jews!

> Mob outside courtyard where
> a convicted Alfred Dreyfus
> was stripped of his insignia
> January 5, 1895
> Paris

How to Treat an Anti-Semite

The proper thing to do was to make him look ridiculous.

> Theodore Roosevelt
> Police Commissioner of New
> York, explaining his
> decision to assign Jewish
> policemen to guard a
> notorious German
> anti-Semitic speaker
> Mid-1890s

HERZL CALLS FOR A JEWISH STATE

The Jewish question exists wherever Jews live in perceptible numbers. Where it does not exist, it is carried by Jews in the course of their migrations. We naturally move to those places where we are not persecuted, and there our presence produces persecution. This is the case in every country, and will remain so, even in those highly civilized—for instance, France—until the Jewish question finds a solution on a political basis. The unfortunate Jews are now carrying the seeds of Anti-Semitism into England; they have already introduced it into America. . . .

The creation of a new State is neither ridiculous nor impossible. . . .

Let the sovereignty be granted us over a portion of the globe large enough to satisfy the rightful requirements of a nation; the rest we shall manage for ourselves.

> Theodor Herzl
> *The Jewish State*
> 1896

FIRST ZIONIST CONGRESS

The aim of Zionism is to create for the Jewish people a home in Palestine secured by public law.

> First Zionist Congress
> Declaration
> Basle, Switzerland
> August 1897

CONCERNING THE JEWS

I am persuaded that in Russia, Austria, Germany, nine-tenths of the hostility toward the Jew comes from the average Christian's inability to compete successfully with the Jew. . . .

If the statistics are right, the Jews constitute but one percent of the human race. It suggests a nebulous dim puff of stardust lost in the blaze of the Milky Way. Properly, the Jew ought hardly to be heard of, but he is heard of, has always been heard of. He is as prominent on the planet as any other people, and his commercial importance is extravagantly out of proportion to the smallness of his bulk. His contributions to the world's list of great names in literature, science, art, music, finance, medicine, and abstruse learning are also away out of proportion to the weakness of his numbers. He has made a marvelous fight in this world, in all the ages, and has done it with his hands tied behind him. . . . The Egyptian, the Babylonian, and the Persian rose, filled the planet with sound and splendor, then faded to dream stuff and passed away. The Greek and the Roman followed, and made a vast noise, and they are gone. . . . The Jew saw them all, beat them all, and is now what he always was, exhibiting no decadence, no infirmities of age, no weakening of his parts, no slowing of his energies, no dulling of his alert and aggressive mind. All things are mortal but the Jew; all other forces pass, but he remains.

> Mark Twain
> *Harper's New Monthly*
> *Magazine*
> September 1898

RIOTS IN FRANCE

Anti-Jewish riots [in the wake of the Dreyfus case] spread throughout France, to some 70 towns and cities; mobs screamed "Death to the Jews" and attacked synagogues, Jewish shops, and Jews on the streets. The police often seemed ineffective, perhaps even in sympathy with the rioters, a situation right out of Russia. . . . Anti-Jewish boycotts were organized, and the anti-Semitic leagues sprang back to life, gaining an unprecedented following.

> Albert S. Lindemann
> Describing events of 1898
> *The Jew Accused*
> 1991

THE BODY AND THE SOUL

When I used to come home . . . bleeding and crying from the wounds inflicted upon me by the Christian boys, my father . . . made me understand that this is only a passing state in history, as we Jews belong to eternity, when God will comfort His people. Thus the pain was only physical, but my real suffering began later in life, when I emigrated from Rumania to so-called civilized countries and found there what I might call the Higher Anti-Semitism, which burns the soul though it leaves the body unhurt.

> Solomon Schechter
> Seminary address
> March 26, 1903

Cited in A Treasury of Jewish Quotations, *edited by Joseph L. Baron.*

ANTI-SEMITIC PUBLICATIONS

From the end of 1905 to 1916 the government [of Czarist Russia] permitted the printing and distribution of over 14 million copies of some 3,000 anti-Semitic books and pamphlets. The czar himself allegedly contributed over 12 million rubles from his private fortune towards the dissemination of hate literature, including *The Protocols of the Elders of Zion.*

Statistics
1905–16

Statistics cited in The Jew Accused *by Albert S. Lindemann, 1991.*

ON THE DISAPPEARANCE OF JEWRY

The assimilation of intelligent Jewry would be for the other races, and the assimilation of poor Jewry would be for its own race, a benefaction, even salvation. The disappearance of Jewry is a presupposition of civilization.

Gustav Ratzenhofer
Soziologie
1907

Cited in The Jews of Germany *by Ruth Gay.*

COMMENT ON BEILIS TRIAL

Never has . . . a trial in Russia . . . attracted, to so great a degree, the attention of the broad masses. . . . The Beilis Affair [alleging a "ritual murder"] has pushed aside all other internal and foreign affairs. . . . [The trial has shown Russians that] the Jewish question is not only a Jewish question but a Russian question; that the untruth and corruption uncovered at the Beilis trial is an all-Russian untruth and corruption.

> Vladimir Korolenko
> Summer 1913
> Kiev

Cited in Blood Accusation *by Maurice Samuel, 1966.*

DOUBLE VERDICT IN BEILIS CASE

[Count one:] Has it been proved [that] . . . in one of the buildings of the Jewish surgical hospital . . . Andrei Yushchinsky was gagged, and wounds inflicted upon him . . . and that after he had lost five glasses of blood . . . leading to almost total loss of blood and to death?
[Verdict:] Yes, it has been proved.
[Count two:] Is the accused [Mendel Beilis] guilty of having entered into collusion with others who have not been discovered . . . in a premeditated plan prompted by religious fanaticism, to murder the boy Andrei Yushchinsky, and did he carry out his intentions?
[Verdict:] No, not guilty.

> Jury verdict
> October 28, 1913
> Kiev

IN THE WAKE OF A TRIAL, ANTI-SEMITISM

At the trial [in Atlanta], jurors heard mobs shouting, "Hang the Jew," through courthouse windows. And after the Jewish factory owner was convicted of killing a young girl and the governor commuted his death sentence to life, the mob did just that, kidnapping Leo Frank from jail and stringing him up from an oak tree 100 miles away near Marietta.

It was perhaps the worst single outburst of anti-Semitism in America: Jews fled Atlanta for Birmingham and beyond, some carrying guns against death threats. Others struggled to survive business boycotts and cold shoulders from friends. The Ku Klux Klan rose again on the little girl's ghost.

> Events in Georgia
> 1913–15

Cited in "Leo Frank and the Winds of Hate" by Art Harris, in the Washington Post, *December 20, 1983.*

MOB ASSAILS COMMUTATION

We want John M. Slaton, King of the Jews and traitor Governor of Georgia!

> Mob chant
> Outside governor's home
>   following commutation of
>   Frank sentence to life
>   imprisonment
> Atlanta
> 1915

COMMENT ON FRANK LYNCHING

In putting the Sodomite murderer [Leo Frank] to death the Vigilance Committee has done what the Sheriff should have done, if [Georgia Governor] Slaton had not been in the mold of Benedict Arnold [by commuting Frank's sentence to life im-

prisonment]. LET JEW LIBERTINES TAKE NOTICE! Georgia is
not for sale to rich criminals.

Tom Watson
Jeffersonian
1915

BALFOUR BACKS NATIONHOOD

His Majesty's Government views with favour the establishment
in Palestine of a national home for the Jewish people, and will
use their best endeavors to facilitate the achievement of this
object, it being clearly understood that nothing shall be done
which may prejudice the civil and religious rights of existing
non-Jewish communities in Palestine, or the rights and political status enjoyed by Jews in any other country.

Arthur J. Balfour
Statement
London
November 2, 1917

BAD NEWS FROM POLAND

Terrible news is reaching us from Poland. The newly liberated
Poles there are trying to get rid of the Jews by the old and
familiar method which they learnt from the Russians [*pogroms*]. Heart-rending cries are reaching us. We are doing all
we can, but we are so weak!

Chaim Weizmann
Letter
November 29, 1918

NEW PARTY ANNOUNCES PROGRAM

The Program of the German Workers Party is a program for our time. . . . Only Nationals can be Citizens of the State. Only persons of German blood can be Nationals. . . . No Jew can therefore be a German National.

Any person who is not a Citizen will be able to live in Germany only as a guest and must be subject to regulation for Aliens. . . .

We demand that the State make it its duty to provide opportunities of employment first of all for its own Citizens. If it is not possible to maintain the entire population of the State, then foreign nationals [those who are not Citizens] are to be expelled from the Reich. . . .

The Party . . . stands for positive Christianity. . . . It fights against the Jewish-materialistic spirit within and around us.

Party Platform
February 24, 1920

NEW PARTY SAYS SWEEP AWAY "JEWISH VERMIN"

There are various views on the ultimate aim and task of the German-National movement regarding the Jews. One believes that so-called explanatory work is all that is needed; the next only wants to "eliminate" the Jewish spirit from the "cultural" field; a third only from the economy, and a fourth has other aims again, and all the opinions become confused. . . . Quite apart from this we consider that it is much more urgent and necessary that the local groups should seek to operate first of all on their home ground and to sweep away Ostjuden [Jews who came to Germany from Eastern Europe] and Jewish vermin in general with an iron broom. . . .

Such measures might be . . . the immediate removal of

Jews from all Government employment, newspaper offices, theaters, cinemas, etc., in short, the Jew must be deprived of all possibilities to continue to make his disastrous influence felt. . . .

> Pamphlet of the National Socialist
> German Workers Party
> March 10, 1920

A Call for Unity

Anti-Semites of the world, unite! People of Europe, free yourselves!

> Adolf Hitler
> Speech
> August 13, 1920

The Opposite of a Panacea

If there were no Jews they would have to be invented, for the use of politicians—they are indispensable, the antithesis of a panacea, guaranteed to *cause* all evil.

> Israel Zangwill
> *Voice of Jerusalem*
> 1921

On Jewish Control

Jews have always controlled the business. . . . The motion picture influence of the United States and Canada . . . is exclusively under the control, moral and financial, of the Jewish manipulators of the public mind.

Dearborn Independent
Published by Henry Ford
February 1921

1922 WHITE PAPER ON PALESTINE

Unauthorized statements have been made to the effect that the purpose in view is to create a wholly Jewish Palestine, "as Jewish as England is English." His Majesty's Government regard any such expectation as impracticable and have no such aim in view. . . . They would draw attention to the fact that the terms of the [Balfour] Declaration referred to do not contemplate that Palestine as a whole should be converted into a Jewish National Home, but that such a Home should be founded *in Palestine. . . .*

Further, it is contemplated that the status of all citizens of Palestine in the eyes of the law shall be Palestinian, and has never been intended that they, or any section of them, should possess any other juridical status.

Winston Churchill
British Colonial Secretary
White paper
1922

FIGHTING JEWS IN THE NAME OF GOD

I believe that I am acting in accordance with the will of the Almighty Creator: by defending myself against the Jew, I am fighting for the work of the Lord.

Adolf Hitler
Mein Kampf
1925

RACE DEFILEMENT

With satanic joy in his face, the black-haired Jewish youth lurks in wait for the unsuspecting girl whom he defiles with his blood, thus stealing her from her people.

> Adolf Hitler
> *Mein Kampf*
> 1925

HITLER AND HATRED

Gradually I began to hate them. . . . For me this was the time of the greatest spiritual upheaval I have ever gone through. I had ceased to be a weak-kneed cosmopolitan and become an anti-Semite.

> Adolf Hitler
> *Mein Kampf*
> 1925

EVALUATING HITLER

Wit, irony, humor, sarcasm, earnestness, passion, white heat—all this is contained in his speech. This man has everything it takes to be king. The great tribute of the people. The coming dictator.

> Joseph Goebbels
> Diary entry
> November 6, 1925
> From *The Goebbels Diaries*

THE BORN AGITATOR

As a speaker he [Hitler] combines gesture, mimicry, and language in great harmony. The born agitator. With that man one can conquer the world. Unleash him and he makes the whole corrupt republic totter.

> Joseph Goebbels
> Diary entry
> June 16, 1926
> From *The Goebbels Diaries*

NAZI LEAFLET

When we have the power of the state in our hands [we] will thoroughly annihilate this international racial parasite.

> Election leaflet
> Nazi party
> 1927–1929

Cited in Ideology of Death *by John Weiss.*

JEWS MASSACRED IN HEBRON

One day in September of that year [1929], on a Sabbath eve, the Arabs of Hebron were brought to a point of such frenzied hatred against the Jews [by the Mufti] that they invaded the synagogue and slaughtered all the men and women at prayer there. . . . After killing the Jews in the synagogue, the Arab mob in Hebron went down the road . . . where stood a yeshivah, a Jewish theological seminary, and massacred both students and professors. . . . After this the mob . . . attacked the house of the local rabbi . . . , where a number of men and women had taken refuge. . . . But the Arabs came in throughout the windows . . . and made short shrift of the 38 persons in the room. Their throats were slit and both men and women were horribly mutilated. . . .

There wasn't a British policeman or a soldier to be seen in all Hebron that night of death.

> Pierre Van Paassen
> Recalling events of 1929
> *A Pilgrim's View*
> 1956

Election Slogan

Germany awake! Death to Judah!

> Nazi Party slogan
> 1930

The Uses of Brutality and Fear

Brutality is respected. The people need wholesome fear. They want to fear something. They want someone to frighten them and make them shudderingly submissive. Haven't you seen everywhere that after the beerhall battles those who have been beaten are the first to join the party as new members? Why babble about brutality and get indignant about tortures? The masses want them. They need something that will give them a thrill of horror.

> Ernst Roehm
> Statement
> Early 1930s

Cited in The Voice of Destruction *by Hermann Rauschning, 1940.*

STALIN ON ANTI-SEMITISM

Anti-Semitism . . . is the most dangerous survival of cannibalism.

> Joseph Stalin
> Statement
> Moscow
> January 12, 1931

INCIDENT AT A BERLIN SCHOOL

A student arrives at school to find a swastika atop a turret of the school building. A man is seen climbing up the turret toward the Nazi flag.

The man up there was Dr. Levy, our French teacher. We recognized him by the empty left sleeve of his jacket that fluttered in the breeze as he groped his way over the roof to the turret, climbed up the fire ladder, swung himself over the railing, and pulled down the swastika flag. . . .

Dr. Levy led our second class period. . . . When the first [chalk]board was filled, he pushed it up to reveal the other slate panel underneath, where he meant to do the last few verbs. But two words were already written on the board, in large block letters: SALOPE JUIF! [Jewish sow]. . . .

Then he took the sponge, wiped away the word SALOPE, and replaced it with a new word. Now the phrase read MANCHOT JUIF. Manchot, we had heard from him, was slang for a veteran who had lost an arm—as he had in 1917 at the Battle of Arras.

> Bernt Engelmann
> *In Hitler's Germany: Daily Life
> in the Third Reich*
> Recalling events of May 30,
> 1932

HOLOCAUST

JANUARY 30, 1933

Adolf Hitler becomes chancellor of Germany.

MARCH 9, 1933

First concentration camp established at
Dachau, outside of Munich.

THE ASSAULTS BEGIN

On March 9th and 10th [1933], bands of Nazis throughout
Germany carried out wholesale raids to inundate the opposition, particularly the Jews. . . . Men and women were in-
sulted, slapped, punched in the face, hit over the heads with
blackjacks, dragged out of their homes in night clothes and
otherwise molested. . . . Never have I seen law-abiding citizens living in such unholy fear.

> Edmond Taylor
> *Chicago Tribune* reporter
> Relating events of March
> 9–10, 1933

Cited in The Jews in Nazi Germany *by the American Jewish Committee.*

NAZIS ORDER BOYCOTT

In every local branch and organizational section of the NSDAP
[Nazi Party] Action Committees are to be formed immediately
for the practical systematic implementation of a boycott of
Jewish shops, Jewish goods, Jewish doctors and Jewish
lawyers. . . .

The Boycott Will Start on April 1!

The boycott is not to begin piecemeal, but all at once; all
preparations to this end are to be made immediately. Orders
will go out to the SA and SS to post guards outside Jewish
stores from the moment that the boycott comes into force, in
order to warn the public against entering the premises.

> *Volkischer Beobachter,* No.
> 88
> March 29, 1933

STREICHER HAILS BOYCOTT

On Saturday, 1 April [1933], at 10 A.M., the German people begins defensive action against the Jewish world-criminals! [A compulsory one-day boycott of Jewish businesses.] National-Socialists! Strike down the world-enemy!

> Julius Streicher
> Article in *Volkischer*
> *Beobachter*
> March 31, 1933

BOYCOTT SIGNS

The Jews are our misfortune.
    A German buys nothing from Jews.

> Nazi boycott signs
> Oberdorf, Germany
> April 1, 1933

"GOLGOTHA HAS NOT YET BEEN AVENGED!"

We have now fought for 14 years for the German people, and now, when we want to give it peace, it is more troubled than ever before. For weeks past, the newspapers abroad have been saying that Bolsheviks caught in Germany were tortured to death, that they had their eyes put out, that their corpses were mutilated and that pogroms were arranged!

    For 14 years we have been repeating in Germany: German

people, learn to recognize your true enemy! And the German simpletons listened carefully and then declared that we preached religious hatred. Now the German people is awake. Yes, the whole world now speaks of the eternal Jew.

Never since the beginning of the world and the creation of man has there been a nation which cared to fight against a nation of bloodsuckers and extortioners who for a thousand years have spread all over the world.

The German people did not wish to start that fight, but one day it will thank the fates for the fact that the eternal Jew had been negligent and had thrown a burning torch amongst the nations. The day will come, when humanity will free itself from the Jewish scourge and will stretch its hands towards the eternal peace. It is only because the German people had not recognized its enemy for so long that such unutterable suffering has overwhelmed us. It was left to our movement to expose the eternal Jew as a mass murderer.

I do not ask you whether you are Catholics or Protestants, but if you are Christians, then I tell you: Golgotha has not yet been avenged. But time brings its own revenge, and those who were responsible for Golgotha are already on their way to it.

> Julius Streicher
> *Muenchener Beobachter*
> Daily supplement to the
>   *Volkischer Beobachter*
> Issue No. 91/92
> April 1/2, 1933

Defining a Non-Aryan

A person is to be considered non-Aryan if he is descended from non-Aryans, and especially from Jewish parents or grandparents. It is sufficient if one parent or grandparent is non-

Aryan. This is to be assumed in particular where one parent or grandparent was of the Jewish religion.

> First Regulation for the
> Implementation of the Law
> for the Restoration of the
> Professional Civil Service
> April 11, 1933

GERMAN JEWS TERRORIZED

An indeterminate number of Jews have been killed. Hundreds of Jews have been beaten or tortured. Thousands of Jews have fled. Thousands of Jews have been, or will be, deprived of their livelihood.

All of Germany's 600,000 Jews are in terror.

> H. R. Knickerbocker
> *New York Evening Post*
> April 15, 1933

APRIL 21, 1933

Nazi law prohibits kosher butchering.

A Reason for Anti-Semitism?

May we ask if Hitler's attitude may be somewhat governed by the fact that too many Jews, at least in Germany, are radical, too many are communists? May that have any bearing on the situation? There must be some reason other than race or creed—just what is that reason? It is always well to try to understand.

The Christian Century
April 26, 1933

At the Burning of the Books

On May 10, 1933, university students in Berlin publicly burned thousands of books seized from both public and private libraries. The books represented both Jewish and non-Jewish writers of many nationalities. They had one thing in common: they displeased the Nazis.

The age of extreme Jewish intellectualism has now ended, and the success of the German revolution has again given the right of way to the German spirit. . . . From these ashes there will rise the phoenix of a new spirit. . . . Brightened by these flames our vow shall be: The Reich and the Nation and our Fuehrer Adolf Hitler: Heil! Heil! Heil!

Joseph Goebbels
Speech
May 10, 1933
From *The Goebbels Diaries*

Are We Being Fair to the Germans?

To deny that Germany can speak as a civilized power because uncivilized things are being said and done in Germany, is in itself a deep form of intolerance. . . . Who that has studied history and cared for the truth would judge the French people by what went on during their terror? Or the British people by what happened in Ireland? Or the Catholic church by the Catholic church of the Spanish Inquisition? Or Protestantism by the Ku Klux Klan or the Jews by their parvenus?

> Walter Lippmann
> Column in *Los Angeles Times*
> May 19, 1933

The Crime Without a Name

One day, in the year 1933, a young Polish lawyer appeared before the Legal Council of the League of Nations in Madrid. The lawyer, whose name was Raphael Lemkin, was appalled by the murder of a million Armenians by Turkey during World War I. He was also shocked by the massacre of Christian Assyrians by Iraq. Lemkin's proposal to the League: draft an international treaty to ban . . . the organized murder of minority groups.

The League—which apparently looked upon Lemkin as some kind of wild-eyed visionary—turned the proposal down cold.

Lemkin went back home to Poland to his job as secretary of the Committee on Codification of the Laws of the Polish Republic.

> Events of 1933
> *Our Age*, Volume 1, No. 3,
> November 29, 1959

In 1944, Lemkin would coin a name for the crime: genocide, *from the Greek word* genos *meaning "race," and the Latin word* cide *meaning "killing."*

INSTRUCTIONS TO AN AMBASSADOR

The German authorities are treating the Jews shamefully and the Jews in this country are greatly excited. But this is not a governmental affair. We can do nothing except for American citizens who happen to be made victims. We must protect them, and whatever we can do to moderate the general persecution by unofficial and personal influence ought to be done.

> Franklin D. Roosevelt
> Instructions to U.S.
>   Ambassador William E.
>   Dodd
> June 1933

From Ambassador Dodd's Diary, 1933–1938, *edited by William E. Dodd, Jr., and Martha Dodd.*

HITLER ON RELIGION

The religions are alike, no matter what they call themselves. They have no future—certainly none for the Germans. Fascism, if it likes, may come to terms with the Church. So shall I. Why not? That will not prevent me from tearing up Christianity root and branch, and annihilating it in Germany. The Italians are naive; they're quite capable of being heathens and Christians at the same time. The Italians and the French are especially heathens. Their Christianity is only skin-deep. But the German is different. He is serious in everything he undertakes. He wants to be either a Christian or a heathen. He cannot be both. Besides, Mussolini will never make heroes of his Fascists. It doesn't matter there whether they're Christians or heathens. But for our people it is decisive whether they acknowledge the Jewish Christ-creed with its effeminate pity-ethics, or a strong, heroic belief in God in Nature, God in our own people, in our destiny, in our blood.

Leave the hair-splitting to others, whether it's the old Testament or the New, or simply the sayings of Jesus, according to Houston Stewart Chamberlain—it's all the same old Jewish swindle. . . .

You can't make an Aryan of Jesus, that's nonsense.

Adolf Hitler
Summer 1933

From The Voice of Destruction *by Hermann Rauschning.*

A "Transfer Agreement"

Negotiated between Nazi Germany and Zionist organizations in the summer of 1933, it [the "Transfer Agreement"] permitted limited Jewish immigration from Germany to Palestine and was intended as a means of rendering Germany *judenrein* (literally, "clean of Jews"). Jewish wealth was confiscated as the price of an exit visa and Hitler thus had no need to soil his hands with Jewish blood at an inopportunely early date. . . .

The Transfer Agreement functioned smoothly up to 1937 and only haltingly thereafter until 1939. From the start, however, it was an object of controversy within the Zionist movement. It is noteworthy that the agreement was concluded by the left-leaning Zionist majority under the leadership of David Ben-Gurion. From the very beginning, the Revisionists of the rightist Zionist opposition, rejected any form of cooperation with Hitler. . . .

Michael Wolffsohn
Eternal Guilt?
Citing events of 1933

STERILIZATION LAW

Anyone who is suffering from a hereditary disease can be sterilized by a surgical operation if, according to the experiences of medical science, it is to be expected with great probability that his offspring will suffer from serious hereditary physical or mental defects. . . .

1. Mental deficiency from birth.
2. Schizophrenia.
3. Circular (manic-depressive) lunacy.
4. Hereditary epilepsy.
5. Hereditary St. Vitus Dance (Huntington's Chorea).
6. Hereditary blindness.
7. Hereditary deafness.
8. Serious hereditary physical malformation.

Furthermore, persons suffering badly from alcoholism can be sterilized.

German Law
July 14, 1933

HALF-JEWISH, AGED 5½

My father said, "Be careful about the men in the brown uniforms." He said, "Be quiet, don't attract attention to yourself, don't look at them and just walk straight." Possibly with your eyes cast down. That was the first intimation I had that something was amiss. I'm not sure I even know why I had to be careful of the men in the brown uniforms. I think my father said they don't like Jews. I don't remember. And from that day on, it was just, I had to be invisible.

Rita Kuhn
Recalling her entrance to
    kindergarten in Berlin
1933

Quoted in Frauen: German Women Recall the Third Reich *by Alison Owings.*

FAREWELL TO SCOUTING

I was a Boy Scout and my life was Scouting. We had seen a lot
of the world—as a boy I was in Poland, Sweden, France, the
Netherlands. But then came 1933. I was then 14. One day the
leader of our Boy Scout group said to me, "I have heard that
your father is a Jew. . . . We are now awaiting word that we
will become part of the *Hitlerjugend* (Hitler youth) and with a
member like you we'll have problems. . . . Think it over. I will
not throw you out, but think it over and tell me if you
agree." . . .

I did not know what this meant—this business about my
father being a Jew. To me he had always looked like Goethe. At
last I went to my father and told him what had happened. He
told me that "if somebody doesn't want you, don't run after
them." And so I left the Scouts.

Werner Goldberg
Interview
Recalling events of 1933

From Special Treatment *by Alan Abrams.*

HOW TO BEHAVE TOWARD JEWS

By the attitude you display toward the Jews you must see to it
that Jewry must never again have even the least influence
among our people. Know your real enemy!

Nazi propaganda sign
Mid–1930s

Cited in Ashkenaz: The German Jewish Heritage, *edited by Gertrude Hirschler.*

A Song for Little Nazis

We love our Fuehrer,
We honor our Fuehrer,
We follow our Fuehrer,
Until men we are,
We believe in our Fuehrer,
We live for our Fuehrer,
We die for our Fuehrer,
Until heroes we are.

Pre-Nursery School
Children's Song
Mid-1930s

Cited in Education for Death *by Gregor Ziemer.*

A U.S. Officer Admires the Nuremberg Rally

[The Nuremberg rally showed us such values as] love of country, democratic indifference to caste, fanatical hatred of Jews and bolshevists and everyone else who differed from the Nazis, and above all the pride in Germany's armed forces.

Lt.-Col. Truman Smith
U.S. Military Attache, Berlin
Report on the Nuremberg
Rally
1935

Cited in "American Diplomats in Berlin (1935–1939) and their Attitude to the Nazi Persecution of the Jews" by Shlomo Shafir, Yad Vashem Studies, *Volume IX, 1973.*

"Life Unworthy of Life"

Prior to Auschwitz and the other death camps, the Nazis established a policy of direct medical killing: that is, killing arranged within medical channels, by means of medical decisions, and carried out by doctors. . . . The Nazis called this program "euthanasia." . . .

The Nazis used this justification for direct medical killing on the simple concept of "life unworthy of life." . . . While the Nazis did not originate this concept, they carried it to its ultimate biological, racial, and "therapeutic" extreme.

Of the five definable steps by which the Nazis carried out the principle of "life unworthy of life," coercive sterilization was the first. There followed the killing of "impaired" children . . . , and then the killing of "impaired" adults, mostly collected from the mental hospitals, in centers especially equipped with carbon monoxide gas. This project was extended . . . to "impaired" inmates of concentration and extermination camps and, finally, to mass killings, mostly of Jews, in the extermination camps themselves.

> Robert Jay Lifton
> *The Nazi Doctors*
> Events of 1935–41

School Lessons

A flood of abusive literature of all types and for all age groups was published and circulated throughout Germany. Illustrative of this type of publication is the book *Der Giftpilz*. This book brands the Jew as a persecutor of the labor class, a race defiler, a devil in human form, a poisonous mushroom, and a murderer. This particular book was used to instruct school children to recognize the Jew by caricatures of his physical features, and to teach them that the Jew abuses little boys and girls, and that the Jewish Bible permits all crimes.

> Citing official publishing
> activities beginning in the
> mid-1930s
> International Military
> Tribunal
> *Nazi Conspiracy and
> Aggression*

INTERMARRIAGES FORBIDDEN

Marriages between Jews and subjects of the state of German or related blood are forbidden. . . . Extramarital intercourse between Jews and subjects of the state of German or related blood is forbidden. Jews may not employ in their households female subjects of the state of German or related blood who are under 45 years old.

> Nuremberg Law for the
> Protection of German
> Blood and German Honor
> September 15, 1935

NEWS FROM GERMANY

HITLER DEPRIVES JEWS OF CITIZENSHIP RIGHTS, BANS INTERMARRIAGES

THREATENS OTHER STEPS TO SOLVE RACE PROBLEM

> *Baltimore Sun*, headline
> September 16, 1935

A British View of German Policy

German policy is clearly to eliminate the Jew from German life, and the Nazis do not mind how this is accomplished. Mortality and emigration provide the means.

> Eric Mills and Frank Foley
> Report to the British
>   Foreign Office
> October 1935

Who Is a Jew?

A Jew cannot be a Reich citizen. He has no voting rights . . . he cannot occupy a public office. . . .

A Jew is a person descended from at least three grandparents who are full Jews by race. . . .

A *Mischling* who is a subject of the state is also considered a Jew if he is descended from two full Jewish grandparents [if] he was a member of the Jewish Religious Community at the time of . . . this Law, or who was married to a Jew at the time of . . . this Law . . . [or] was born from a marriage with a Jew . . . [or] was born as the result of extramarital intercourse with a Jew . . . and was born illegitimately after July 31, 1936.

> First Regulation to the
>   Reich Citizenship Law
> November 14, 1935

A NAZI PICTURE BOOK

DON'T TRUST THE FOX IN THE GREEN MEADOW

NOR THE JEW ON HIS OATH

A picture book for grownups and little ones. . . .

Jesus Christ says, "The Jew is a murderer through and through." And when Christ had to die the Lord didn't know any other people who would have tortured him to death, so he chose the Jews. That is why the Jews pride themselves on being the chosen people. . . .

[Illustration shows the Jewish butcher.] He sells half-refuse instead of meat. A piece of meat lies on the floor, the cat claws another. This doesn't worry the Jewish butcher since the meat increases in weight. Besides, one mustn't forget, he won't have to eat it himself. . . .

[Illustration] What a poor specimen the Jew is. He doesn't like his own women and thinks himself clever if he steals a German woman for himself. Yet look at the Jew: He doesn't even fit her. . . .

[Illustration shows Streicher as friend and educator of German boys and girls.] We have a fighter in the German Gau of Franconia whom we have to thank that our country remains healthy and free of Jewish residue.

[Illustration shows German children reading the *Stuermer*.] Dirty Jews! . . .

[Illustration shows expulsion of Jewish children from the school whilst German children jeer.] Now it is going to be nice at school, for all Jewish children have to go, big ones and little ones. Crying, weeping, fury and anger doesn't help. Away with the Jewish brood!

Elvira Bauer, author
Published by the printing
department of *Der
Stuermer*
1936

HISTORY UNITS IN GERMAN HIGH SCHOOL

The German worker under Jewish influence; influence of Marx; class hatred; influence of the Jews on the press, theater, books; the Treaty of Versailles and its evils; Germany's freedom under Hitler; Hitler working toward world peace.

Mid-1930s.

Cited in Education for Death, *by Gregor Ziemer.*

SAYING "NO" TO HEIDELBERG

The academic world owes it to this once great university . . . to let the German government know just what its feelings are toward the treatment of the German university by the Nazis [regarding dismissal of Jewish professors].

University of Virginia
Statement turning down an
   invitation to help
   celebrate the 550th
   anniversary of the
   University of Heidelberg
Charlottesville, Virginia
April 1936

A Suicide at the League of Nations

I do not find any other way [than suicide] to reach the hearts of men . . . [because of the] inhuman indifference of the world.

> Stefan Lux
> Suicide note addressed to
>   Anthony Eden, British
>   Cabinet Minister for
>   League of Nations Affairs
> July 3, 1936

Lux committed suicide in the press gallery of the League's assembly room.

Policies Doom Europe's Jews

[There are] six million doomed, for whom the world is divided into places they cannot leave and places into which they cannot enter.

> Chaim Weizmann
> Statement to the British
>   Royal Commission in
>   Jerusalem
> 1936

The Two Faces of Germany

. . . by the summer of 1936, when the Germany which was host to the Olympic games was enchanting the visitors from the West, the Jews had been excluded either by law or by Nazi terror—the latter often preceded the former—from public and private employment to such an extent that at least one half of them were without means of livelihood. . . . In many towns the Jew found it difficult if not impossible to purchase food. Over the grocery and butcher shops, the bakeries and the dairies, were signs, "Jews Not Admitted." . . . Pharmacies would not sell them drugs or medicine. . . . And always, wherever they went, were the taunting signs "Jews Strictly Forbidden in This Town" or "Jews Enter This Place at Your Own Risk." At a sharp bend in the road near Ludwigshafen was a sign, "Drive Carefully! Sharp Curve! Jews 75 Miles an Hour!"

> William L. Shirer, in
> *The Rise and Fall of the*
> *Third Reich*
> Germany 1936

GERMANY DRESSES UP FOR THE OLYMPICS

The Olympic games held in Berlin in August 1936 afforded the Nazis a golden opportunity to impress the world with the achievements of the Third Reich, and they made the most of it. The signs *"Juden Unerwuenscht"* (Jews Not Welcome) were quickly hauled down from the shops, hotels, beer gardens, and places of public entertainment, the persecution of Jews . . . temporarily halted and the country put on its best behavior.

> William L. Shirer, in
> *The Rise and Fall of the*
> *Third Reich*
> Events of August 1936

A TIME TO SPEAK

No more are we ready to keep silent at man's behest when God commands us to speak. We must obey God rather than man!

> Rev. Martin Niemoeller
> Ca. 1937

Cited in Louis L. Snyder's Historical Guide to World War II, *1982.*

STREICHER ON HOLY WORKS

The Holy Scripture is a horrible criminal romance abounding with murder, incest, fraud and indecency. . . .
    The Talmud is the great Jewish book of crimes that the Jew practices in his daily life.

> Julius Streicher, in
> *Der Stuermer*
> April 1937

"RITUAL MURDER" PROPAGANDA

The numerous confessions made by the Jews show that the execution of ritual murders is a law to the Talmud Jew. The former chief rabbi, and later monk, Teofite, declared that the ritual murders take place especially on the Jewish Purim in memory of the Persian murders, and Passover in memory of the murder of Christ. The instructions are as follows:
    "The blood of the victims is to be tapped by force. On Passover it is to be used in wine and matzos. Thus, a small part

of the blood is to be poured into the dough of the matzos and into the wine. The mixing is done by the Jewish head of the family. The procedure is as follows:

"The family head empties a few drops of the fresh and powdered blood into the glass, wets the fingers of the left hand with it and sprays (blesses) with it everything on the table. The head of the family says, 'Thus we ask God to send the ten plagues to all enemies of the Jewish faith.' Then they eat, and at the end, the head of the family exclaims, 'May all Gentiles perish, as the child whose blood is contained in the bread and wine.'

The fresh, or dried and powdered blood of the slaughtered is further used by young married Jewish couples, by pregnant Jewesses, for circumcision and so on. Ritual murder is recognized by all Talmudic Jews. The Jew believes he absolves himself thus of his sins.

Der Stuermer
April 1937

A GUIDE FOR TEACHING ABOUT JEWS

How should we represent the Jew to our pupils? Only one answer can be given to this question: "In all his monstrosity, horror and dangerousness. . . ."

A teacher who has come to a thorough understanding of the Jewish question will make use in his work of the *Stuermer*. He reads to the class extracts from an article which describes how a Jew deceived a peasant, etc. . . .

Our fight against the Jew is not for the reason that he is different in body to ourselves. The bodily difference is not the dangerous part of the Jew. We must make it clear to a child that in the strange appearance of a Jew, which is immediately conspicuous to us, lies a soul, which is fundamentally different in all its emotions and manifestations, from our souls. We must point out that the Jew thinks, feels, and behaves in a different manner from ourselves. That his way of thinking, of feeling and of behavior is diametrically opposite to our morals and our laws. . . .

Jewry is Criminality

But the fact that, in deceit, usury, murder, etc., Jews see no crime but consider them as acts pleasing to their God when they are directed against non-Jews—will appear most monstrous to our children. At first it will frighten the children and they will shake their heads incredulously. In the same way as millions of people in Germany scornfully shook their heads when the national socialists and foremost of all the *Stuermer* exposed the criminal methods and criminal laws of the Jews.

But deceit, usury, falsehood are sins. A boy in the class will cry out, "We are forbidden to commit them!" The teacher will ask, "Who forbade you to commit them?: "Our conscience. The laws of the State, God."

But if deceit, usury, falsehood, etc., are not crimes, not sin in the eyes of the Jews, then a Jew must have a different conscience, and a different God than we have, and thus the teacher and his pupils will suddenly find themselves thoroughly involved in the Jewish question and in its most serious aspect. The manner in which he (the teacher) pursues the question with the children should make clear to them the fundamental reason for all Jewish acts.

One who has reached this stage of understanding, will inevitably remain an enemy of the Jews all his life and will instill the hatred into his own children.

Fritz Fink, Municipal School
Inspector
From the pamphlet, *The
Jewish Question and
School Instruction*
Published by *Der Stuermer*
1937

Introduced into evidence at Nuremberg.

JEWS AND GERMAN CULTURE

The hatred which breaks out from time to time against the Jews . . . is the impossible attempt to oust from . . . German culture . . . the very element which enlightens, gives form, is human.

> Thomas Mann
> Speech
> April 18, 1937

A PLACE FOR THE LOW ROAD

It is the historical merit of the *Stuermer* to have enlightened the broad masses of our people in a popular way as to the Jewish world danger. The *Stuermer* is right in refusing to fulfill its task in the tone of the aesthetic drawing room. Jewry has shown no regard for the German people. We have, therefore, no cause to be considerate and to spare our worst enemy. What we fail to do today our youngsters of tomorrow will have to suffer for bitterly. Heil Hitler.

> Baldur von Schirach, Reich
>   Youth Leader
> Letter to *Der Stuermer*
> January 1938

MARCH 13, 1938

Anschluss: Hitler takes over Austria.

ALL THEIR FAULT

Do you think the persecution of Jews in Europe has been their own fault?

Entirely	12%
Partly	49%
Not at all	23%
No opinion	16%

Charles Herbert Stember
Survey
Jews in the Mind of America
March 1938

ITALIAN FASCISTS' DECLARATION

The majority of the Italian population is of Aryan origin and its civilization is Aryan. . . . Jews do not belong to the Italian race. They are the only ethnic group that has never assimilated itself with the rest of the Italian population because it is composed of racial elements who are not European, and are totally different from those elements who have given the world the Italian race.

Fascist Party
Declaration
March 1938

AMERICAN POLL ON REFUGEES

An Opinion Research Corporation poll in March 1938, the month of the Austrian Anschluss [Nazi takeover of Austria], found only 17 percent agreeable to admission of "a larger number of Jewish exiles from Germany" (75 percent opposed, 8 percent had no opinion).

> Events of March 1938
> David S. Wyman, in *Paper Walls*

TERROR IN PROGRESS

All or most [German and Austrian Jews] are thrown into concentration camps, committing suicide, and those who still hold out are subjected to humiliation and torture.

> Chaim Weizmann
> Letter to Sir Warren Fisher
> April 19, 1938

A VISION AND A PROPHECY

Part of us will be destroyed and on their bones New Judea may arise! It is all terrible, but it is so.

> Chaim Weizmann
> Letter to Blanche Dugdale
> July 7, 1938

EVIAN AND "INVOLUNTARY EMIGRATION"

Considering that the question of involuntary emigration has assumed major proportions and that the fate of the unfortunate people affected has become a problem for intergovernmental deliberation:

Aware that the involuntary emigration of large numbers of people, of different creeds, economic conditions, professions and trades, from the country or countries where they have been established, is disturbing to the general economy, since these persons are obliged to seek refuge, either temporarily or permanently, in other countries at a time when there is serious unemployment; that, in consequence, countries of refuge and settlement are faced with problems, not only of an economic and social nature, but also of public order, and that there is a severe strain on the administrative facilities and absorptive capacities of the receiving countries;

Aware, moreover, that the involuntary emigration of people in large numbers has become so great that it renders racial and religious problems more acute, increases international unrest, and may hinder seriously the processes of appeasement in international relations;

Believing that it is essential that a long-range program should be envisaged, whereby assistance to involuntary emigrants, actual and potential, may be co-ordinated within the framework of existing migration laws and practices of Governments.

Considering that if countries of refuge or settlement are to co-operate in finding an orderly solution of the problem . . . they should have the collaboration of the country of origin . . . that it will make its contribution by enabling involuntary emigrants to take with them their property and possessions and emigrate in an orderly manner. . . .

Recommends . . .

That the Governments participating in the Intergovernmental Committee shall continue to furnish the Committee for its strictly confidential information, with: 1) details regarding such immigrants as each Government may be prepared to receive under its existing laws and practices and 2) details of these laws and practices;

That in view of the fact that the countries of refuge and settlement are entitled to take into account the economic and social adaptability of immigrants, these should in many cases be required to accept at least for a time, changed conditions of living in the countries of settlement;

That the Governments of the countries of refuge and settlement should not assume any obligations for the financing of involuntary emigration;

That, with regard to the documents required by the countries of refuge and settlement, the Governments represented on the Intergovernmental Committee should consider the adoption of the following provision:

In those individual immigration cases in which the usually required documents emanating from foreign official sources are found not to be available, there should be accepted such other documents serving the purpose of the requirements of law as may be available to the immigrant . . .

That there should meet at London an Intergovernmental Committee consisting of such representatives as the Governments participating in the Evian Meeting may desire to designate. This Committee shall continue and develop the work of the Intergovernmental Meeting at Evian . . . There shall be a director of authority. . . . He shall undertake negotiations to improve the present conditions of exodus and to replace them by conditions of orderly emigration. He shall approach the Governments of the countries of refuge and settlement with a view to developing opportunities for permanent settlement. . . .

The Intergovernmental Committee, at its forthcoming meeting at London, will consider the scale on which its expenses shall be apportioned among the participating Governments. . . .

> Evian conference report
> Evian, France
> July 14, 1938

A DELEGATE AT EVIAN

It will no doubt be appreciated that as we have no racial problem, we are not desirous of importing one.

> T. W. White, Australian
> delegate to the Evian
> Conference
> July 1938

Changing Names

Insofar as Jews have given names other than those which they are permitted to bear . . . they are required . . . to take an additional given name, males will take the given name Israel, females the given name Sara.

> Regulation Requiring Jews
> to Change Their Names
> August 17, 1938

Planning to Destroy a Synagogue

At a meeting in Nurnberg, before the representatives of the German press, [Julius] Streicher and Mayor Liebel of Nurnberg revealed in advance to the gathered members of the press that the Nurnberg synagogue was to be destroyed. The minutes of this meeting dated 4 August 1938, read as follows:
"The breaking up of the synagogue"
[information must still be secret]
"On August 10, 1938 at 10 o'clock A.M., the breakup of the synagogues will commence. Gauleiter Julius Streicher will personally set the crane into motion with which the Jewish symbols, Star of David, etc., will be torn down. This should be arranged in a big way. Closer details are still unknown."
Streicher himself supervised the demolition, according to a newspaper account of 11 August 1938, which described the scene:
"In Nurnberg the Synagogue is being demolished; Julius Streicher himself inaugurates the work by a speech lasting more than an hour and a half. By his order then—so to speak as a prelude of the demolition—the tremendous Star of David came off the cupola."

> Events of August 1938
> *Nazi Conspiracy and*
> *Aggression*
> International Military
> Tribunal
> 1946

ANTI-SEMITISM AND CHRISTIANITY

Anti-Semitism is . . . a movement in which we, as Christians, cannot have any part whatever . . . Spiritually, we are Semites.

Pope Pius XI
September 1938

SEPTEMBER 29, 1938

Sellout at Munich, as British and French agree to turn over Czech territory to Hitler.

NOVEMBER 7, 1938

Herschel Grynzpan, a young Jew, shoots German diplomat Ernst Vom Rath at the German embassy in Paris. Upon Vom Rath's death, the Nazis set off a series of pogroms throughout Germany. The night of November 9–10 will become known as *Krystallnacht* (Crystal Night)—the night of broken glass.

INSTRUCTIONS FOR A POGROM

Only such measures are to be taken as do not endanger German lives or property (i.e., synagogues are to be burned down only where there is no danger of fire in neighboring buildings).

Places of business and apartments belonging to Jews may be destroyed but not looted . . .

In commercial streets particular care is to be taken that non-Jewish businesses are completely protected against damage . . .

As soon as the course of events during the night permits . . . as many Jews in all districts—especially the rich—as can be accommodated in existing prisons are to be arrested. For the time being only healthy male Jews, who are not too old, are to be detained. After the detention has been carried out the appropriate concentration camps are to be contacted immediately for the prompt accommodation of the Jews in the camps. Special care is to be taken that the Jews arrested . . . are not ill-treated.

> Reinhard Heydrich
> Telegram
> November 10, 1938

SPEER: THE MORNING AFTER

On November 10, driving to the office, I passed by the still smoldering ruins of the Berlin synagogues. . . . This memory is one of the most doleful of my life, chiefly because what really disturbed me at the time was the aspect of disorder that I saw on Fasanenstrasse: charred beams, collapsed facades, burned-out walls. . . . Most of all I was troubled by the political revival of the "gutter."

I did not see that more was being smashed than glass, that

on that night Hitler had crossed a Rubicon . . . had taken a step that irrevocably sealed the fate of his country. Did I sense, at least for a moment, that something was beginning which would end with the annihilation of one whole group of our nation? Did I sense that this outburst of hoodlumism was changing my moral substance? I do not know.

I accepted what had happened rather indifferently. . . . I felt myself to be Hitler's architect. Political events did not concern me. My job was merely to provide impressive backdrops for such events.

> Albert Speer
> Recollection of November
> 10, 1938, Berlin

From his memoirs Inside the Third Reich, *1970.*

THE OUTCOME OF *KRISTALLNACHT*

   200   Synagogues destroyed
   700   Jewish businesses destroyed
   200   Jews murdered
35,000   Jews arrested and sent to concentration camps [1,000 of whom will be dead within three months]

> November 1938

Statistics from Ideology of Death *by John Weiss.*

PRESS REACTION TO CRYSTAL NIGHT

No man can look on the scenes witnessed yesterday without shame for the degradation of his species.

> *The New York Times*

The outside world, which has fully appraised the iron discipline of National Socialism, can draw but one conclusion— that the outrages committed by those mobs were winked at if not actually approved, by the governing authorities.

Herald Tribune, New York

Humanity stands aghast and ashamed at the indecency and brutality that is permitted in Germany.

Post-Standard, Syracuse, New York

The people outside Germany who still value tolerance, understanding, and humanity, can no more keep silent in the face of what has just taken place than they would in the face of any other barbarity.

Courant, Hartford, Connecticut

A pogrom hardly surpassed in fury since the Dark Ages. . . . Not on the basis of such savagery can there be any hope of understanding between the leaders of Germany and the people of this country. Britain will be revolted to a man by this sadistic outbreak.

News Chronicle, London

No foreign propagandist bent upon blaspheming Germany before the world could outdo the tale of burnings and beatings, of blackguardly assaults upon defenceless and innocent people, which disgraced that country yesterday.

The Times, London

Germany has delivered herself over to an orgy of savagery which will send a thrill of horror throughout the civilised world. . . . Nazi revenge is one of the most terrible things of the present century.

Daily Telegraph, London

Editorials
November 1938

Cited in Krystallnacht *by Anthony Read and David Fisher.*

NOVEMBER 12, 1938

Nazis prohibit Jewish attendance at movies, concerts, plays, or exhibitions.

GOERING: "I'D HATE TO BE A JEW IN GERMANY"

One more question, gentlemen. What would you think the situation would be if I'd announce today that Jewry shall have to contribute this one billion [marks] as a punishment.

I shall choose the wording this way: that German Jewry shall, as punishment for their abominable crimes, etc., etc., have to make a contribution of one billion; that'll work. The pigs won't consider another murder. I'd hate to be a Jew in Germany.

> Hermann Goering
> Chairing a meeting at the
>   Air Ministry following the
>   Crystal Night destruction
> November 12, 1938

A CRACKDOWN ON TRADE

From January 1, 1939, Jews . . . are forbidden to operate retail stores, mail-order houses, or sales agencies, or to carry on a trade independently. They are further forbidden . . . to offer for sale goods or services, to advertise these, or to accept orders at markets of all sorts, fairs or exhibitions. . . .

Where a Jew is employed in an executive position in a commercial enterprise he may be given notice to leave in six weeks. . . . all claims of the employee based on his contract, especially those concerning pension and compensation rights, become invalid.

> Hermann Goering
> Decree
> Plenipotentiary for the
>   Four Year Plan
> November 12, 1938

JEWS FINED A BILLION MARKS

The hostile attitude of Jewry toward the German People and Reich, which does not even shrink from cowardly murder, calls for determined resistance and severe expiation. . . .

The totality of Jews who are German subjects will pay a [fine] of one billion Reichmarks to the German Reich.

> Hermann Goering
> Decree
> November 12, 1938

LINDBERGH PONDERS CRYSTAL NIGHT

The *Times* [of London] carries a long account of the Jewish troubles in Germany. I do not understand these riots on the part of the Germans. It seems so contrary to their sense of order and their intelligence in other ways. They have undoubtedly had a difficult Jewish problem, but why is it necessary to handle it so unreasonably?

> Charles A. Lindbergh,
> journal entry
> November 13, 1938

Cited in The Wartime Journals of Charles A. Lindbergh.

APPEAL FROM A RADIO COMMENTATOR

Every Jew in Germany was held responsible for this boy's [Herschel Grynszpan's] deed. In every city an organized and

methodical mob was turned loose on the Jewish population. . . . But in Paris, a boy who had hoped to make some
gesture of protest which would call attention to the wrongs
done his race burst into hysterical sobs. . . . he realized that
half a million of his fellows had been sentenced to extinction
on the excuse of his deed. . . .

If any Jews, anywhere in the world, protest at what is
happening, further oppressive measures will be taken. . . .
Therefore, we who are not Jews must speak, speak our sorrow
and indignation and disgust in so many voices that they will be
heard.

                                        Dorothy Thompson
                                        Radio broadcast
                                        November 14, 1938

Cited in Krystallnacht, *by Anthony Read and David Fisher.*

ROOSEVELT RECALLS AMBASSADOR

The news of the last few days from Germany has deeply
shocked public opinion in the United States. Such news from
any part of the world would inevitably produce a similar
profound reaction among American people in every part of the
nation. I myself could scarcely believe that such things could
occur in a 20th-century civilization. . . .

With a view to gaining a first-hand picture of the current
situation in Germany, I asked the Secretary of State to order
our ambassador in Berlin to return at once for report and
consultation.

                                        Franklin D. Roosevelt
                                        Press conference
                                        Washington, D.C.
                                        November 15, 1938

Mayor Comments on "Nazi Guardian Squad"

Purely routine, purely routine.

> Mayor Fiorello H. LaGuardia
> of New York City
> Statement to reporters after
> announcing creation of a
> special police unit to
> guard the Nazi consulate
> Every member of the unit
> was a Jew
> November 1938

A Serious Setback for Anti-Semitism

The good prospects for a gradual spread of anti-Semitism had suffered a serious setback. . . . Yesterday in an old Protestant church in Massachusetts, they went so far as to have a rabbi preach for the first time, departing from a 300-year-old tradition, in order to show that in a situation like the present they stand by the Jews.

> Hans Heinrich Dieckhoff,
> German Ambassador to
> the U.S.
> Message to Berlin
> November 1938

German Ambassador Contacts Berlin

Until November 10 . . . large and powerful sections of the American people had still remained aloof from this [anti-Nazi] campaign . . . partly out of sympathy for the Third Reich, in which they saw a stronghold of order and a bulwark against riots and against unlawful encroachments against private property. Today, this is no longer the case. . . . The fact that Jewish newspapers write still more excitedly than before and that the Catholic bishops campaign against Germany is still waged more bitterly than before is not surprising; but, that men like Dewey, Hoover, Hearst, and many others who have hitherto maintained comparative reserve and had even, to some extent, expressed sympathy toward Germany, are now publicly adopting so violent and bitter an attitude against her is a serious matter. One central theme runs through all these utterances, and a trusted American friend characterized it as follows: "It is generally felt, even among well-wishers of Germany, that the recent events are the best thing that could have happened to the Jews because they arouse universal sympathy, and the worst thing that could have happened to Germany. It jeopardizes the appeasement that was to follow Munich."

> Hans Heinrich Dieckhoff,
> German Ambassador to
> the U.S.
> Message to Berlin
> November 1938

GOEBBELS ON THE GERMAN JEWS

We do not wish to export anti-Semitism. On the contrary, we want to export the Semites! If the whole world were anti-Semitic, how should we get rid of the Jews? We would like the whole world to become so friendly to the Jews that it would absorb all our German Jews.

> Joseph Goebbels
> Speech
> November 20, 1938

Sympathy Yes, Admission No

In November 1938, in the midst of American and world protest against events of the week of Broken Glass, the question [on admission of "a larger number of Jewish exiles from Germany"] drew a . . . favorable response of 21 percent (71 percent opposed; 8 percent had no opinion).

> Events of November 1938
> David S. Wyman, in *Paper Walls*

A Solution to the Jewish Question

. . . No power in the world can stop us, we shall therefore now take the Jewish Question towards its solution. The program is clear. It is: total elimination, complete separation! . . .

It means not only the elimination of the Jews from the German national economy . . . The Jews must . . . be driven out of our apartment houses and residential areas and put into series of streets or blocks of houses where they will be together and have a little contact as possible with Germans.

Once this nation of parasites is in every way dependent on itself and isolated, it will become impoverished . . .

> *Das Schwarze Korps*
> SS publication
> November 24, 1938

Comment on Lost Driving Privileges

With this measure of defense against Jewish arrogance [banning Jews from owning or driving motor cars], the National Socialist state has given new expression to the feeling of justice of the German people. The German man has long felt it as a provocation and as an impediment to public life that Jews can sit at the steering wheel of a motor car in the traffic of German streets, or should profit by the roads of Adolf Hitler that German labor has created. This situation, until now tolerated by the German people with incredible patience, has now reached its end. Jews in Germany can no longer sit at the wheel of a car. Instead, the working German man will have more opportunity than hitherto by means of the motor car, to the work of German intelligence and German hands, of learning to know the beauties of his homeland and of acquiring new strength for his labor.

> *Borsen Zeitung*
> Editorial
> December 1938

On Jewish Children and History

If I knew that all Jewish children could be saved from Germany by being transferred to England, whereas only half of them could be saved if transferred to Eretz Israel, I would choose the second alternative, since the problem, in my opinion, is not only one concerning the children, but a historical issue of the Jewish people.

> David Ben-Gurion
> Mapai meeting
> December 7, 1938

Sign at Ford Motor Plant

Jews Teach Communism

Jews Teach Atheism

Jews Destroy Christianity

Jews Control the Press

Jews Produce Filthy Movies

Jews Control Money

> Sign at Employee Gate
> Ford Motor Company
> Dearborn, Michigan
> 1939

From Henry Ford and the Jews *by A. Lee.*

POLL TURNS THUMBS DOWN ON REFUGEES

A Gallup poll in early 1939 found only 26 percent approval for possible legislation for entry of 10,000 German refugee children (66 percent opposed, 8 percent had no opinion).

> Events of early 1939
> David S. Wyman, in *Paper Walls*

A CHILLING PROPHECY

One thing I should like to say on this day which may be memorable for others as well as for us Germans: In the course of my life I have very often been a prophet, and have usually been ridiculed for it. During the time of my struggle for power it was in the first instance the Jewish race which only received my prophecies with laughter when I said that I would one day take over the leadership of the State, and with it that of the whole nation and that I would then among many other things settle the Jewish problem. Their laughter was uproarious, but I think that for some time now they have been laughing on the other side of their face. Today I will once more be a prophet: If the international Jewish financiers in and outside Europe should succeed in plunging the nations once more into a world war, then the result will not be the bolshevization of the earth, and the victory of Jewry, but the annihilation* of the Jewish race in Europe!

> Adolf Hitler
> Speech
> January 30, 1939

PANIC IN THE STREETS

Everyone who can manage it is trying to get out of the country [Germany]. It's not easy to get an emigration visa; it almost seems as if all the countries had conspired to make emigration difficult for the German Jews. In one, they restrict immigration; in another, they forbid it altogether. Urgent applications are delayed, important letters lie unanswered. Affidavits are mislaid; sponsorships have to be begged for. A person with no connections abroad, no influential sponsors, must resign himself to staying here as an unwelcome alien. *Sauve qui peut!* [Stampede! Panic!]

> Ruth Andreas-
> Friedrich
> Diary excerpt
> February 24, 1939

From Berlin Underground *by Ruth Andreas-Friedrich.*

Editor's Note: Translating scholars have given several different variations of this word, including "extermination" and "obliteration." German translators at the time of the speech tended to use the word "end." Considering the history, the latter word is probably as meaningful as any.

MARCH 15, 1939

Hitler takes over all of Czechoslovakia.

1939 WHITE PAPER ON PALESTINE

The Royal Commission and previous Commissions of Enquiry have drawn attention to the ambiguity of certain expressions in the Mandate, such as the expression "a national home for the Jewish people," and they have found in this ambiguity and the resulting uncertainty as to the objectives of Arabs and Jews. His Majesty's Government are convinced that in the interests of the peace and well-being of the whole people of Palestine a clear definition of policy and objectives is essential. The proposal of partition recommended by the Royal Commission would have afforded such clarity, but the establishment of self-supporting independent Arab and Jewish States within Palestine has been found to be impracticable. It has therefore been necessary for His Majesty's Government to devise an alternative policy . . .

CONSTITUTION. . . . The objective of His Majesty's Government is the establishment within ten years of an independent Palestine State . . . in which Arabs and Jews share in government. . . .

IMMIGRATION. . . . It has been urged that all further Jewish immigration into Palestine should be stopped forthwith. . . . His Majesty's Government are conscious of the present unhappy plight of large numbers of Jews who seek a refuge from certain European countries, and Palestine can and should make a further contribution to the solution of this pressing world problem. . . . Jewish immigration during the next five years will be at a rate which, if economic absorptive capacity permits, will bring the Jewish population up to approximately one-third of the total population of the country. . . . This would allow of admission . . . of some 75,000 immigrants over the next five years. . . . In addition, as a contribution to the solution of the Jewish refugee problem, 25,000 refugees will be admitted as soon as the High Commissioner is satisfied that adequate provision for their maintenance is ensured. . . .

LAND. . . . The Reports of several expert Commissions have indicated that, owing to the natural growth of the Arab population and the steady sale in recent years of Arab land to Jews, there is now in certain areas no room for further transfers of Arab land, whilst in some other areas such transfers of land must be restricted if Arab XKKC are to maintain their existing standard of life and a considerable landless Arab population is not soon to be created. In these circumstances, the High Commissioner will be given general powers to prohibit and regulate transfers of land.

British Government
White Paper
London
May 17, 1939

JEWISH AGENCY ATTACKS WHITE PAPER

It [the white paper] puts up a territorial ghetto for Jews in their own homeland. . . .

The Mandatory has decided to reward the terrorists by surrendering the Jewish National Home. . . .

It is in the darkest hour of Jewish history that the British Government proposes to deprive the Jews of their last hope and to close the road back to their Homeland. It is a cruel blow, doubly cruel because it comes from the government of a great nation which has extended a helping hand to the Jews, and whose position must rest on foundations of moral authority and international good faith.

Jewish Agency for Palestine
Statement
1939

AN APPEAL FOR THE ST. LOUIS REFUGEES

I appeal to you [Cuban President Batista] because of your well-known feeling for the victims of German Nazism. If returned to Germany, these people will undoubtedly be sent to Nazi concentration camps.

> John L. Lewis
> Cable
> *The New York Times*
> June 2, 1939

There were more than 1,100 German Jewish refugees on board the ship St. Louis, fleeing from Hitler. They were in Havana harbor. Some 700 of them had immigration quota numbers which would have allowed them to enter the United States in 1942. Only 22 Jews were allowed to land in Havana. The rest were returned to Europe. A few hundred lucky Jews were accepted in Britain, where most survived the war. The vast majority, who were given refuge in France, Belgium, and Holland, were destined for eventual Nazi deportation—and death.

CHAMBERLAIN ON THE NAZI PERSECUTION

I believe the persecution arose out of two motives: a desire to rob the Jews of their money and a jealousy of their superior cleverness. . . . No doubt Jews aren't a lovable people; I don't care about them myself; but that is not sufficient to explain the Pogrom.

> Neville Chamberlain
> Letter
> July 30, 1939

AUGUST 23, 1939

Nazi Germany and Soviet Union sign
non-aggression pact.

SEPTEMBER 1, 1939

Hitler invades Poland, setting off
World War II.

Nazis Establish Jewish Councils

SECRET

Special Delivery Letter
To The Chiefs of task forces of the Security Police.
Concerning: The Jewish problem in the occupied zone. . . .

(1) In each Jewish community a Council of Jewish Elders is to be set up which, as far as possible, is to be composed of the remaining influential personalities and rabbis. The Council is to be composed of 24 male Jews (depending on the size of the Jewish community).

The Council is to be made fully responsible (in the literal sense of the word) for the exact execution according to terms of all instructions released or yet to be released.

(2) In case of sabotage of such instructions, the Councils are to be warned of severest measures.

(3) The Jewish Councils are to take an improvised census of the Jews of their area, possibly divided into generations (according to age)—

a. up to 16 years of age,

b. from 16–20 years of age, and

c. those above and also according to the principal vocations—and they are to report the results in the shortest possible time.

(4) The Councils of Elders are to be made acquainted with the time and date of evacuation, the evacuation possibilities, evacuation routes. They are, then, to be made personally responsible for the evacuation of the Jews from the country [side].

The reason to be given for the concentration of the Jews to the cities is that Jews have most decisively participated in sniper attacks and plundering.

(5) The Councils of Elders of the concentration centers are to be made responsible for the proper housing of the Jews to be brought in from the country. The concentration of Jews in the cities for general reasons of security will probably bring about orders to forbid Jews to enter certain wards of the cities altogether, and that in consideration of economic necessity

they cannot, for instance, leave the ghetto, they cannot go out after a designated evening hour, etc.

(6) The Councils of Elders are also to be made responsible for the adequate maintenance of the Jews on the transport to the cities.

No scruples are to be voiced if the migrating Jews take with them all their movable possessions, as far as that is technically at all possible.

(7) Jews who do not comply with the order to move into cities are to be given a short additional period of grace when there is good reason. They are to be warned of strictest penalty if they should not comply by the appointed time.

Reinhard Heydrich
Berlin
September 21, 1939

Cited in Judenrat: The Jewish Councils in Eastern Europe Under Nazi Occupation by Isaiah Trunk.

SEPTEMBER 23, 1939

Jews in Germany may no longer own radios.

HEADLINES FROM THE JEWISH CHRONICLE

FORCIBLE EXODUS: NAZIS SEND THOUSANDS TO LUB-
LIN; GHETTO-STATE OF 4 MILLION?

> Headline
> *The Jewish Chronicle*
> London
> November 10, 1939

MASS MURDER IN POLAND:
THREE THOUSAND SUICIDES; BURIALS DAY AND NIGHT

> Headline
> *The Jewish Observer*
> London
> December 15, 1939

"ANNIHILATING POLISH JEWRY": NAZIS BOASTED AIM;
OVER 120,000 VICTIMS ALREADY;

NAZI ATROCITIES CONFIRMED;
MASS SLAUGHTER OF POLISH JEWS

> Headline
> *The Jewish Chronicle*
> London
> January 12, 1940

WEARING STARS OF DAVID

All Jews and Jewesses within the Government-General [occu-
pied Poland] who are over ten years of age are required,
beginning December 1, 1939, to wear on the right sleeve of

their inner and outer garments a white band at least 10 cm wide, with the Star of David on it.

> Regulation for the
>   Identification of Jewish
>   Men and Women
> November 23, 1939

JEWISH COUNCILS ESTABLISHED

1. In each community a body representing the Jews will be formed.

2. This representation of the Jews, known as the Judenrat, will consist of 12 Jews in communities with up to 10,000 inhabitants, and in communities with more than 10,000 inhabitants, of 24 Jews, drawn from the locally resident population. The Judenrat will be elected by the Jews of the community. If a member of the Judenrat leaves, a new member is to be elected immediately.

3. The Judenrat will elect a chairman and a deputy from among its members.

4. After these elections, which must be completed not later than December 31, 1939, the membership of the Judenrat is to be reported to the responsible [official]. . . .

5. It is the duty of the Judenrat through its chairman or his deputy to receive the orders of the German Administration. It is responsible for the conscientious carrying out of orders to their full extent. The directives it issues to carry out these decrees must be obeyed by all Jews and Jewesses.

> Governor General of
>   Occupied Polish
>   Territories
> Decree
> Cracow, Poland
> November 28, 1939

No Railroads

The use of the Railroad by Jews is prohibited until further notice. This does not apply to journeys for which there is an order in writing from the Governor General, his office, or of a District Commander.

> Regulation for the Use of the
> Railroad in the Government-
> General [Occupied Poland]
> January 26, 1940

We're Not Perfect

We, as Americans, do not have the moral right to judge what is happening. After all, we are not perfect ourselves.

> Anne Morrow Lindbergh
> Statement
> 1940
> Quoted in *Holocaust and
> Genocide*

Pornography as a Metaphor

They [Allied leaders] treat us [Jews] as a pornographical subject. Pornography covers a most important department of life and nature; nobody denies it, but you cannot discuss it in polite society—it is not done.

> Arthur Szyk
> In *The Jewish War Front,*
> Vladimir Jabotinsky
> 1940

JEWS IN A RESTORED POLAND

Restored Poland will deal with Jews left within her gates exactly as she pleases.

There is every reason to fear that it may soon become politically awkward to insist on promises of real equality for the Jews in a Poland restored by an Allied victory. Nazi propaganda in the German-occupied section of the republic is sure to seize upon such undertakings as a useful means of making the Polish government in exile unpopular with Poles in Poland. One can almost anticipate the very wording of the broadcasts and articles which Dr. Goebbels' headquarters will devote to the subject: "They promise you restoration, but their first step is to be the reinstatement of the two million Jews in those economic positions from which the German victory has driven them, so that two million Poles will have to make room for these Jews and starve."

Racial peace in Poland—and not in Poland only—will be possible only as a corollary to a very extensive, and very greatly accelerated repatriation of Jewish masses to whatever spot on earth they may consider their national homeland.

Vladimir Jabotinsky
The Jewish War Front
1940

WINROD SEES ANTI-SEMITISM RISE

A wave of anti-Semitism is sweeping the world as a reaction against (1) Jewish control of news channels, (2) international Jewish banking, and (3) atheistic Communism, which was originally spawned in Jewish capitalism and Jewish intellectualism.

Rev. Gerald B. Winrod
1940

Cited in Christian Beliefs and Anti-Semitism *by Charles Y. Glock and Rodney Stark.*

CATASTROPHE WITHOUT PARALLEL

The gigantic catastrophe which has descended on Polish Jewry has no parallel, even in the darkest periods of Jewish history. First, in the depth of the hatred. This is not hatred whose source is simply in a party platform, invented for political purposes. It is a hatred of emotion, whose source is some psychopathic disease. In its outward manifestations it appears as physiological hatred, which sees the object of its hatred as tainted in body, as lepers who have no place in society. The masses have accepted this sort of objective hatred. . . .They have absorbed their masters' teaching in a concrete bodily form. The Jew is filthy; the Jew is a swindler and evil, . . . the Jew is Satan.

> Chaim A. Kaplan
> Diary excerpt
> Warsaw
> March 10, 1940

From Scroll of Agony: The Warsaw Ghetto Diary of Chaim A. Kaplan, *1973.*

A "BRUTAL, VICIOUS WAR"

[Germany is waging] one of the basest, most brutal and vicious wars in human history . . . the war of extermination against the Jewish people of Germany.

> *Buffalo Courier Express*
> Editorial
> April 6, 1940

JUNE 22, 1940

France signs armistice with Nazi Germany.

JULY 29, 1940

German Jews may no longer have telephones.

THE MADAGASCAR PROPOSAL

The approaching victory gives Germany the possibility, and in my view also the duty, of solving the Jewish question in Europe. The desirable solution is: all Jews out of Europe. . . .

In the Peace Treaty France must make the island of Madagascar available for the solution of the Jewish question, and to resettle and compensate the approximately 25,000 French citizens living there. The island will be transferred to Germany under a mandate. . . . The Jews will be jointly liable for the value of the island. For this purpose their former European financial assets will be transferred for use to a European bank to be established to pay for the land which they will receive, and for the purpose of necessary commodities in Europe for the development of the island. . . .

This arrangement would prevent the possible establishment in Palestine by the Jews of a Vatican State of their own, and the opportunity for them to exploit for their own purposes the symbolic importance which Jerusalem has for the Christian and Mohammedan parts of the world. Moreover, the Jews will remain in German hands as a pledge for the future good behavior of the members of their race in America.

Franz Rademacher
Memorandum
Berlin
July 3, 1940

"JEWS MUST VANISH"

It is clear that herewith, a serious warning must be given—the Jews must vanish from the face of the earth.

> Hans Frank
> Speech
> Reported on CBS World
>   News
> Berlin
> August 19, 1940

Cited in Inside the Vicious Heart *by Robert H. Abzug, 1985.*

ALL IN A SINGLE YEAR

The first anniversary of the outbreak of the war.

In this year of torments, Polish Jewry has been destroyed. Its property and holdings were confiscated; all sources of income were blocked; its ancient communities were uprooted and exiled; its cemeteries are piles of rubble; its human rights have been erased and annulled; its lives are worthless. Imprisoned, subjugated, and mummified in the narrow confines of ghettos, it is declining to the lowest level of human survival. . . . Spiritual life is paralyzed. All the libraries, academies, and other buildings which were a haven for the Jewish spirit have been destroyed, and still the enemy is poised to torment us until we disappear from the earth entirely. . . .

All of this in a single year.

> Chaim A. Kaplan
> Diary excerpt
> Warsaw
> September 1, 1940

From Scroll of Agony: The Warsaw Diary of Chaim A Kaplan, *1973.*

On the Advantages of Anti-Semitism

That we were opponents of the Jews was generally known throughout the world, even before 1933. We have, therefore, in any case reaped the disadvantages of anti-Semitism in world propaganda; hence we can afford to enjoy the advantages too, and displace the Jews. Since we are being opposed and calumniated throughout the world as enemies of the Jews, why should we derive only the disadvantages and not also the advantages, i.e., the elimination of the Jews from the theater, the cinema, public life and administration. If we are then still attacked as enemies of the Jews we shall at least be able to say with a clear conscience: It was worth it, we have benefited from it.

> Joseph Goebbels
> Statement
> Propaganda ministerial
>   conference
> Berlin
> September 1940

Warsaw Quarter Established

A Jewish quarter is to be formed in the city of Warsaw. . . . The quarter will be set off from the rest of the city by the following streets. . . .

> Dr. Ludwig Fischer, Governor
> Decree
> October 2, 1940

HANS FRANK REGRETS

Of course, I could not eliminate all lice and Jews in only a year's time. But in the course of time, and above all, if you will help me, this end will be attained.

> Hans Frank
> Diary excerpt
> ca. October 1940

PRICELESS POSSESSION

We are trailed and hunted. We can no longer find a place to hide. Our money is gone. We cannot stay here any longer because we have been threatened with being reported to the Gestapo. If this happens, our protector will suffer as well. We cannot commit suicide in this place because our protector will be victimized. So we have decided to surrender, in the knowledge that we can swallow the (suicide) pills that now constitute our only, our priceless possession.

> Francisca Rubinlicht
> Suicide note
> Warsaw
> ca. early 1940s

Quoted in Their Brothers' Keepers *by Philip Friedman.*

ABOUT THIS MASTER RACE BUSINESS

The crown of all wrongly-applied Rooseveltian logic is the sentence, "There never was a race and there never will be a race which can serve the rest of mankind as a master."

Here . . . we can only applaud Mr. Roosevelt. Precisely because there exists no race which can be the master of the rest of mankind, we Germans have taken the liberty to break the domination of Jewry and of its capital in Germany, of Jewry which believed [itself] to have inherited the crown of secret world domination.

Hans Fritzsche
Radio speech
March 18, 1941

Monitored and translated by the British Broadcasting Corporation.

SOLVING THE JEWISH PROBLEM

The Jewish question will be solved for Europe only when the last Jew has left the European continent.

Alfred Rosenberg
World Struggle
April 1941

VICHY RATIONALE FOR ANTI-JEWISH LAWS

Neither hatred nor reprisals, simply the strict defense of the national interest.

Xavier Vallat
Press conference
Vichy, France
April 1941

Upon the establishment by the French government of the Commissariat for Jewish Questions.

JUNE 22, 1941

Nazi Germany invades Soviet Union.

THE BEGGARS

On Karmelicka Street, near the Evangelical Hospital, stands a beggar whose clothes are impeccable; he has a pretty child with him who is clean and spotless; he begs not with outstretched hand but with his eyes alone. The children constitute the majority of the beggars. . . . Whole choirs of children sing in the street to large audiences.

> Emmanuel Ringelblum
> *Notes from the Warsaw
> Ghetto*
> Early 1940s

WHO, ME?

The bolshevist agitators make no effort to deny that in towns, thousands, in the villages, hundreds, of corpses of men, women and children have been found, who had been either killed or tortured to death. Yet the bolshevik agitators allege that this was not done by Soviet commissars but by German soldiers. Now we Germans know our soldiers. No German woman, father or mother requires proof that their husband or their son cannot have committed such atrocious acts.

> Hans Fritzsche
> Radio speech
> July 10, 1941

Monitored and translated by the British Broadcasting Corporation.

GOERING CALLS ON HEYDRICH

I herewith commission you [Reinhard Heydrich] to carry out all preparations with regard to . . . a total solution of the

Jewish question in those territories of Europe which are under German influence. . . . I furthermore charge you to submit to me as soon as possible a draft showing the . . . measures already taken for the execution of the intended final solution of the Jewish question.

> Hermann Goering
> Directive
> July 31, 1941

HIMMLER WITNESSES A MASSACRE

As the firing started, Himmler became more and more nervous. At each volley, he looked down at the ground. . . . The other witness was Obergruppenfuhrer von dem Bach-Zelewsky. . . . Von dem Bach addressed Himmler: "Reichsfuhrer, those were only a hundred. . . . Look at the eyes of the men in this commando, how deeply shaken they are. These men are finished for the rest of their lives. What kind of followers are we training here? Either neurotics or savages."

> Raul Hilberg
> *The Destruction of the*
> *European Jews*
> Minsk
> Late summer, 1941

ZYKLON B COMES TO AUSCHWITZ

The gassing [of Soviet prisoners-of-war] was carried out in the detention cells of Block 11. Protected by a gas mask, I watched

the killing myself. In the crowded cells, death came instanta-
neously the moment the Zyklon B was thrown in. A short,
almost smothered cry, and it was all over. . . .

I must even admit that this gassing set my mind at rest, for
the mass extermination of the Jews was to start soon, and at
that time neither Eichmann nor I was certain as to how these
mass killings were to be carried out. It would be by gas, but we
did not know which gas and how it was to be used. Now we
had the gas, and we had established a procedure.

> Rudolf Hoess
> Testimony at his war crimes
>   trial
> Events of September 3, 1941

LINDBERGH CITES WARMONGERS

I spoke for 25 minutes. It seemed that over 80 percent of the
crowd was with us by the time I finished; but the ice had been
well broken before I started, by the previous speakers. When I
mentioned the three major groups agitating for war—the
British, the Jewish, and the Roosevelt Administration—the
entire audience seemed to stand and cheer. At that moment
whatever opposition existed was completely drowned out by
our support.

Dozens of people came to our hotel rooms after the
meeting—America First members and supporters and advis-
ers, local officials, newspapermen, etc. Some were solid, stable
citizens; some erratic; some intelligent; some stupid; all types
are present at these meetings, but on the whole we have a
much better than average cross section of the communities
where we meet. Our opposition press, of course, picks out and
emphasizes the radical and fanatical types who attend. They
had more success at doing this, however, before the Communists threw their support to the interventionist cause after war

started between Germany and Russia. We were thankful to be rid of the Communist support which we never wanted and always tried to avoid.

> Charles A. Lindbergh
> Journal entry
> September 11, 1941

Cited in The Wartime Journals of Charles A. Lindbergh.

THE TASK OF THE SONDERKOMMANDO

The investigation of and struggle against tendencies and elements hostile to the Reich, insofar as they are not a part of a hostile military force is, in the occupied areas, exclusively the task of the Sonderkommando of the Security Police and the SD, which will take the necessary measures on their own responsibility and carry them out. Individual actions by members of the Wehrmacht or participation by members of the Wehrmacht in excesses by the Ukrainian population against the Jews is forbidden; they are also forbidden to watch or take photographs of measures taken by the Sonderkommando.

> Gerd von Rundstedt
> Order
> Headquarters, Army Group
>   South
> Occupied Soviet Union
> September 24, 1941

WHO ARE THE WARMONGERS?

The international Jewish-Democratic Bolshevistic campaign of incitement against Germany still finds cover in this or that fox's lair or rat-hole. We have seen only too frequently how the defeats suffered by the warmongers only doubled their senseless and impotent fury.

Hans Fritzsche
Radio speech
October 9, 1941

Monitored and translated by the British Broadcasting Corporation.

A New "Euthanasia" Program

In 1941, I received an order to discontinue the euthanasia program [in Germany]. In order to retain the personnel that had been relieved of these duties and in order to be able to staff a new euthanasia program after the war, Bouhler asked me—I think after a conference with Himmler—to send this personnel to Lublin and place it at the disposal of SS Brigadefuhrer Gobocnik.

Viktor Brack
Testimony at war crimes
trial
Events of 1941

Cited in Belzec, Sobibor, Treblinka *by Yitzhak Arad.*

Defiance from the Pulpit

ANNOUNCEMENT: An inflammatory pamphlet anonymously attacking the Jews is being disseminated among the houses of Berlin. It declares that any German who, because of allegedly false sentimentality, aids the Jews in any way, be it only through a friendly gesture, is guilty of betraying his people. Do not allow yourselves to be confused by this un-Christian attitude, but act according to the strict commandment of Jesus Christ: "Thou shalt love thy neighbor as thyself."

> Dean Bernhard
> Llichtenberg
> Cathedral of St. Hedwig,
> Berlin
> October 1941

ARRANGING POGROMS IN THE BALTIC STATES

To our surprise it was not easy at first to set in motion an extensive pogrom against the Jews. Klimatis, the leader of the partisan unit . . . who was used for this purpose primarily, succeeded in starting a pogrom on the basis of advice given to him by a small advanced detachment active in Kowno and in such a way that no German order or German instigation was noticed from outside. During the first pogrom in the night from 25 to 26 June [1941] the Lithuanian partisans did away with more than 1,500 Jews, setting fire to several synagogues or destroying them by other means and burning down a Jewish dwelling district consisting of about 60 houses. During the following nights about 2,300 Jews were made harmless in a similar way. . . .

It was possible, though, through similar influences on the Latvian auxiliary to set in motion a pogrom against the Jews also in Riga. During this pogrom all synagogues were destroyed and about 400 Jews were killed.

> SS Brigade Fuehrer
> Stahlecker
> Report to Heinrich Himmler
> October 15, 1941

Death Penalty for Leaving

Jews who leave without authorization the district assigned for their residence [in occupied Poland] will suffer the death penalty. The same penalty will apply to persons who knowingly give shelter to such Jews.

> Regulation for Restrictions
> of Residence
> October 15, 1941

Headlines from the Jewish Chronicle

GHASTLY POGROMS IN UKRAINE:
THOUSANDS OF CORPSES IN RIVER DNIESTER:
8,000 SLAIN IN SYNAGOGUES

> Headline
> *The Jewish Chronicle*
> London
> October 24, 1941

ALMOST ONE THIRD OF THE ENTIRE POPULATION OF BESSARABIA WAS EXTERMINATED

> Headline
> *The Jewish Chronicle*
> London
> November 7, 1941

A Pogrom in Sluzk

The first lieutenant explained that the police battalion had received the assignment to effect the liquidation of all Jews here in the town of Sluzk, within two days. Then I requested him to postpone the action one day. However he rejected this with the remark that he had to carry out this action everywhere and in all towns and that only two days were allotted for Sluzk. Within these two days, the town of Sluzk had to be cleared of Jews by all means. . . . All Jews without exception were taken out of the factories and shops and deported in spite of our agreement. It is true that part of the Jews was moved by way of the ghetto where a large part was loaded directly on trucks and liquidated without further delay outside of the town. . . . For the rest, as regards the execution of the action, I must point out to my deepest regret that the latter bordered already on sadism. The town itself offered a picture of horror during the action. With indescribable brutality on the part of both the German police officers and particularly the Lithuanian partisans, the Jewish people, but also among them White Ruthenians, were taken out of their dwellings and herded together. Everywhere in the town shots were to be heard and in different streets the corpses of shot Jews accumulated. The White Ruthenians were in greatest distress to free themselves from the encirclement. Regardless of the fact that the Jewish people, among whom were also tradesmen, were mistreated in a terribly barbarous way in the face of the White Ruthenian people, the White Ruthenians themselves were also worked over with rubber clubs and rifle butts. There was no question of an action against the Jews any more. It rather looked like a revolution.

> Report to Berlin from the
> Commissioner General of
> Sluzk
> White Ruthenia
> October 30, 1941

Cited in evidence at Nuremberg.

Nazi Slogan for a Ghetto

Die Stadt die Hitler den Juden geshenkt hat.
"The town which Hitler gave to the Jews."

Slogan for the Terezin
"Model" Ghetto
In Czechoslovakia
Established in November
1941

Cited in Fragments of Memory *by Hana Greenfield, 1992.*

Warsaw Ghetto Humor

Churchill invited the Chassidic rabbi of Ger to come to see and advise him how to bring about Germany's downfall. The rabbi gave the following reply: There are two possible ways, one involving natural means, the other supernatural. The natural means would be if a million angels with flaming swords were to descend on Germany and destroy it. The supernatural would be if a million Englishmen parachuted down on Germany and destroyed it.

Emmanuel Ringelblum
*Notes from the Warsaw
Ghetto*
ca. 1941

A Hundred Suicides a Day

Jewish suicides are continuing at a rate of over 100 per day throughout the Reich and the numerous reports received of such suicides in Berlin alone indicate that this figure is not implausible.

> Leland Morris
> Telegram to the U.S.
>   Secretary of State
> November 16, 1941

HITLER ADDRESSES THE GRAND MUFTI

The Fuehrer [told the Grand Mufti] that Germany's fundamental attitude . . . was clear. Germany stood for uncompromising war against the Jews. That naturally included active opposition to the Jewish national home in Palestine, which was nothing other than a center, in the form of a state, for the exercise of destructive influence by Jewish interests. . . . Germany was resolved, step by step, to ask one European nation after the other to solve its Jewish problem, and at the proper time direct a similar appeal to non-European nations as well.

> Hitler to Grand Mufti of
>   Jerusalem
> Berlin
> November 28, 1941

WHAT TO DO WITH FRENCH JEWS?

Send them where? Back home, that is to say throughout the whole vast world? By what means, so long as the war is going on? In reality, it will be the victor's business, if he intends to organize a durable peace, to find the means, worldwide if possible, European in any case, to settle the wandering Jew.

> Xavier Vallat
> Preface to *Juif ou Francais*
> by Gabriel Malglaive
> End of 1941

Cited in Vichy France and the Jews *by Michael R. Marrus and Robert O. Paxton.*

GENOCIDE AND THE LABOR SHORTAGE

For the personal information of the Chief of the Industrial Armament Department I am forwarding a total account of the present situation in the Reichskommissariat Ukraine in which the difficulties and tensions encountered so far and the problems which give rise to serious anxiety are stated with unmistakable clarity.

Intentionally I have desisted from submitting such a report through official channels or to make it known to other departments interested in it because I do not expect any results that way. . . .

Jewish problem:

Regulation of the Jewish question in the Ukraine was a difficult problem because the Jews constituted a large part of the urban population. We therefore have to deal—just as in the General Government—with a mass problem of policy concerning the population. Many cities had a percentage of Jews exceeding fifty percent. Only the rich Jews had fled from the German troops. The majority of Jews remained under German administration. The latter found the problem more complicated through the fact that these Jews represented almost the entire trade and even a part of the manpower in small and medium industries besides the business which had in part become superfluous as a direct or in direct result of the war. The elimination therefore necessarily had far-reaching economic consequences and even direct consequences for the armament industry (production for supplying the troops).

The attitude of the Jewish population was anxious— obliging from the beginning. They tried to avoid everything that might displease the German administration. That they hated the German administration and army inwardly goes without saying and cannot be surprising. However, there is no proof that Jewry as a whole or even to a greater part was implicated in acts of sabotage. Surely there were some terrorists or saboteurs among them just as among the Ukrainians. But it cannot be said that the Jews as such represented a danger to the German armed forces. The output produced by Jews who, of course, were prompted by nothing but the feeling of fear, was satisfactory to the troops and the German administration.

The Jewish population remained temporarily unmolested shortly after the fighting. Only weeks, sometimes months later, specially detached formations of the police executed a planned shooting of Jews. The action as a rule proceeded from east to west. It was done entirely in public with the Ukrainian militia, and unfortunately in many instances also with members of the armed forces taking part voluntarily. The way these actions, which included men and old men, women, and children of all ages were carried out was horrible. The great masses executed make this action more gigantic than any similar measure taken so far in the Soviet Union. So far about 150,000 to 200,000 Jews may have been executed. In the part of the Ukraine belonging to the Reichskommisariat, no consideration was given to the interest of the economy.

Summarizing, it can be said that the kind of solution of the Jewish problem applied in the Ukraine which obviously was based on the ideological theories as a matter of principle had the following results:

(a) Elimination of a part of partly superfluous eaters in the cities.
(b) Elimination of a part of the population which hated us undoubtedly.

(c) Elimination of badly needed tradesmen who were in many instances indispensable even in the interests of the armed forces. . . .

(d) Consequences as to foreign policy propaganda which are obvious.

(e) Bad effects on the troops which in any case get indirect contact with the executions.

(f) Brutalizing effect on the formations which carry out the execution—regular police.

> German Armament Inspector in the Ukraine
> Letter to the General of the Infantry, Thomas,
> Chief of the Industrial Armaments Department
> December 2, 1941

DECEMBER 7, 1941

Japanese attack on Pearl Harbor brings the
United States into the war.

"They Must Be Done Away With"

As far as the Jews are concerned, I want to tell you quite frankly that they must be done away with in one way or another. The Fuehrer said once: "Should united Jewry again succeed in provoking a world-war, the blood of not only the nations which have been forced into the war by them, will be shed, but the Jew will have found his end in Europe."

I know that many of the measures carried out against the Jews in the Reich at present are being criticized. It is being tried intentionally, as is obvious from the reports on the morale, to talk about cruelty, harshness, etc. Before I continue, I want to beg you to agree with me on the following formula: We will principally have pity on the German people only, and nobody else in the whole world. The others, too, had no pity on us. As an old National Socialist, I must say: This war would only be a partial success if the whole lot of Jewry would survive it, while we would have shed our best blood in order to save Europe. My attitude towards the Jews will, therefore, be based only on the expectation that they must disappear. They must be done away with. I have entered negotiations to have them deported to the East. A great discussion concerning that question will take place in Berlin in January, which I am going to delegate the State Secretary Dr. Buehler. That discussion is to take place in the Reich Security Main Office with SS Lt.General Heyidrich. [See "A Meeting at Wannsee" on page 124.] A great Jewish migration will begin, in any case. But what should be done with the Jews? Do you think they will be settled down in the "Ostland," in villages? This is what we were told in Berlin: Why all this bother? We can do nothing with them. . . . So liquidate them yourself.

Gentlemen, I must ask you to rid yourself of all feeling of pity. We must annihilate the Jews, wherever we find them and wherever it is possible. . . . This will naturally be achieved by other methods than those pointed out by Bureau Chief Dr. Himmel. Nor can the judges of the Special Courts be made responsible for it, because of the limitations of the framework of the legal procedure. Such outdated views cannot be applied to such gigantic and unique events. We must find at any rate a way which leads to the goal, and my thoughts are working in that direction.

The Jews represent for us also extraordinarily malignant gluttons. We have now approximately 2,500,000 of them in the General Government [of Poland], perhaps with the Jewish mixtures and everything that goes with it, 3,500,000 Jews. We cannot shoot or imprison those 3,500,000 Jews, but we shall nevertheless be able to take measures, which will lead, somehow, to their annihilation, and this in connection with the gigantic measures to be determined in discussions from the Reich. The General Government must become free of Jews, the same as the Reich. Where and how this is to be achieved is a matter for the offices which we must appoint and create in due course.

Hans Frank
Cabinet meeting
Cracow, Poland
December 16, 1941

On Furniture and Hostages

Document Memorandum for the Fuehrer—Concerning Jewish Possessions in France:

In compliance with the order of the Fuehrer for protection of Jewish cultural possessions, a great number of Jewish dwellings remained unguarded. Consequently, many furnishings have disappeared because a guard could, naturally, not be posted. In the whole East the administration has found terrible conditions of living quarters, and the chances of procurement are so limited that it is not practical to procure any more. Therefore, I beg the Fuehrer to permit the seizure of all Jewish home furnishings of Jews in Paris, who have fled or will leave shortly, and that of Jews living in all parts of the occupied West, to relieve the shortage of furnishings in the administration in the East. . . .

A great number of leading Jews were, after a short examination in Paris, again released. The attempts on the lives of members of the armed forces have not stopped; on the contrary, they continue. This reveals an unmistakable plan to disrupt the German-French cooperation, to force Germany to retaliate, and, with this, evoke a new defense on the part of the French against Germany. I suggest to the Fuehrer that, instead of executing 100 Frenchmen, we substitute 100 Jewish bankers, lawyers, etc. It is the Jews in London and New York who incite the French communists to commit acts of violence, and it seems only fair that the members of this race should pay for this. It is not the little Jews, but the leading Jews in France, who should be held responsible. That would tend to awaken the Anti-Jewish sentiment.

> Alfred Rosenberg
> Memorandum to Hitler
> December 18, 1941

An Unpleasant Fate

The fate of Jewry in Europe has turned out as unpleasant as the Fuehrer predicted in the case of a European war. After the extension of the war instigated by Jews, this unpleasant fate may also spread to the New World, for you can hardly assume that the nations of this New World will pardon the Jews for the misery of which the nations of the Old World did not absolve them.

> Hans Fritzsche
> Radio speech
> December 18, 1941

Monitored and translated by the British Broadcasting Corporation.

THE RABBIS AT SACHSENHAUSEN

Many of the Jewish prisoners who bore their ordeal with extraordinary patience became embittered at the brutal treatment of the rabbis. Sometimes they gave vent to their indignation, but in return they were lashed and thrown into solitary confinement. Others cried like children when they had to witness the inhuman cruelties to which the rabbis were subjected. But even crying excited the Nazis, who meted out additional beatings, since everything connected with religion seemed to upset them particularly. Prisoners of all faiths were beaten up if they showed any sympathy for the rabbis or priests, or even if they pronounced the name of the Lord.

> Dr. Leo Stein
> "Rabbis in Sachsenhausen"
> *National Jewish Monthly*
> January 1942

A CALL FOR RESISTANCE

Doubters! Cast off all illusions. . . . Hitler aims to destroy all the Jews of Europe. The Jews of Lithuania are fated to be the first in line.

Let us not go as sheep to the slaughter! . . .

It is better to fall as free fighters than to live by the grace of the murderers.

Resist! To the last breath.

> Jewish Pioneer Youth
>   Group
> Proclamation
> Vilna Ghetto, Lithuania
> January 1, 1942

A Thirst for Books

The Jewish book stores are no more. The stores were closed down, the books removed. The remains of those books that were salvaged from Swientojerska Street, where Jewish book dealers were active for generations, are now being sold out in the street. . . .

Foreign-language books are very popular, especially those in English, since every one is assiduously studying English, in preparation for emigrating after the war. . . .

Polish books are being sold on Leszno Street, Yiddish and Hebrew books on Nowolipki and Zamenhofa Streets, and elsewhere. Of late, one notices the sale of Talmudic volumes— completely unprecedented. Such volumes used formerly to be regarded as holy and translated as a family inheritance from generation to generation.

> Emmanuel Ringelblum
> *Notes from the Warsaw
> Ghetto*
> ca. 1942

The Final Solution

In the course of the final solution, the Jews should be brought under appropriate direction in a suitable manner to the East for labor utilization. Separated by sex, the Jews capable of work will be led into these areas in large labor columns to build roads, whereby doubtless a large part will fall away through natural reduction.

The inevitable final remainder which doubtless constitutes the toughest element will have to be dealt with appropriately, since it represents a natural selection which upon liberation is to be regarded as a germ cell of a new Jewish development. . . .

In the course of the practical implementation of the final

solution, Europe will be combed from West to East. If only because of the apartment shortage and other socio-political necessities, the Reich area—including the Protectorate of Bohemia and Moravia—will have to be placed ahead of the line [for the evacuation of Jews].

For the moment, the evacuated Jews will be brought bit by bit to so-called transit ghettos from where they will be transported further to the east.

> Reinhard Heydrich
> Statement at Wannsee
> Conference
> January 20, 1942

A Meeting at Wannsee

The meeting opened with the announcement by . . . Heydrich of his appointment . . . as Plenipotentiary for the Preparation of the Final Solution of the European Jewish Question. . . . The aim of this task was to cleanse the German living space of Jews in a legal manner. . . . Emigration has now been replaced by evacuation of the Jews to the East. . . . In the course of this final solution . . . approximately 11 million Jews may be taken into consideration. . . . In conclusion, there was a discussion of the various possible forms which the solution might take. . . . Certain preparatory work . . . should be carried out locally in the area concerned, but . . . in doing so, alarm among the population must be avoided.

> Protocol of the Wannsee
> Conference
> January 20, 1942

"Complete Annihilation"

The war will not end as the Jews imagine it will, namely with the uprooting of the Aryans, but the result of this war will be the complete annihilation of the Jews. . . . The hour will come when the most evil universal enemy of all time will be finished, at least for a thousand years.

> Adolf Hitler
> Speech
> January 30, 1942

How to Collect Jewish Skulls

After the Jew has been put to death, without in any way injuring his skull, the physician severs the head from the trunk and sends it to its place of destiny in an hermetically closed tin box, especially adapted to this purpose, filled with a preserving solution. As soon as the dispatch is received by the scientific laboratory, it will be possible to record on a photographic plate the results of comparative and anatomic examinations of the skull, to define racial features as well as the pathological features based on the shape of the skull, the shape and size of the brain, etc., to make measurements and obtain a number of other data regarding the head as well as the skull itself.

> Testimony at war crimes trial
> Proposal for collecting skulls
> of a "sub-human" race
> February 1942

The program was set up at the Natzweiler concentration camp near Strasburg, France.

Memo to the Nuncio

1. The multiplicity of measures, dictated by violent anti-Semitism, which have been taken in the past few years against

the Jews living in Germany and the territories annexed to Germany are more or less well known to public opinion. They consist in the absolute exclusion of Jews from all professions, all trades and all economic activity in general, except for incorporation in the system of forced labor adopted to meet the needs of war. They consist also in the confiscation of almost all the Jews' worldly goods and, in countless cases, of persecution in various forms, such as arrest, internment in concentration camps or mass expulsion of Jews—stripped in advance of all they possess—either to Poland or to concentration camps in France. Through the forced emigration which was pursued up to the outbreak of the war and by reason of the privation and persecution they have endured, the number of German and Austrian Jews has fallen from around 800,000 to about 200,000. . . .

2. Analogous measures, less rigorous in certain cases but even more rigorous in others, have fallen upon the Jews in all the countries occupied during the war by the German Army . . . , notably Poland, where concentration of masses of Jews in ghettos surrounded by unscalable walls has created indescribable misery and caused epidemics which, at this moment, are literally decimating the population.

3. Germany's allies, initiating the example set by the Reich, have followed the same course and introduced anti-Semitic legislation, or launched violent persecution, aimed at the total dispossession or even the physical extermination of the Jews. This is notably the case in Romania, in the newly created states of Croatia and Slovakia and, to a certain degree too, in Hungary, where preparations are now afoot to incorporate all Jews from 18 to 50 in forced labor units.

4. Among the most striking illustrations of such persecution, we would quote the following:

a. The establishment in Occupied France of reprisal camps at Drancy and Compiegne, near Paris, where approximately 6,000 to 7,000 Jews, who were arrested in the streets or in their own homes in August last, are literally dying of hunger and being used by the military authorities as hostages.

b. The establishment of concentration camps in Unoccupied France; for example, at Gurs, at Recebedou, at Noe, Verner, Rivesaltes, etc., where several tens of thousands of Jews of all nationalities, who were already living in France or took refuge in France in consequence of the advance of the German armies into Belgium, have been herded—the women and children separated from their husbands and fathers—into sordid huts surrounded by barbed wire, where they have been vegetating for more than two years in unimaginable misery. To these camps, Germany has also sent 9,000 German Jews who had been established for centuries in Baden and the Palatinate. . . .

c. Among the cruelties perpetrated in the occupied countries by Germany, we would cite the example of several hundred young Dutch Jews who, without any charges being leveled against them, were sent to the concentration camps at Buchenwald in Germany and Mauthausen in Austria, where virtually all of them perished within a few weeks.

d. Apart from the slow and steady extermination associated with the ghetto system throughout Poland, thousands of Jews in Poland and the parts of Russia occupied by Germany have been executed by German troops.

e. Eighteen thousand Jews located in Hungary (a number of whom were Hungarian Jews, the others, Jews of different nationalities) have been expelled by order of the government and transported in revolting conditions to Eastern Galicia, where they were delivered into the hands of the German authorities who shot them all, with few exceptions.

f. Early last year, at the time of the Iron Guard uprising in Romania, several thousand Jews were massacred in the streets of Romanian localities. In Bucharest alone, nearly 3,000 persons—intellectuals, officials of Jewish institutions, merchants and industrialists of repute—were killed. Revolting scenes were enacted, notably at the abattoir in Bucharest, to which the Iron Guard dragged the Jews and there slaughtered them like cattle.

g. Most of the Jews in Bucovina, numbering 170,000, were forced to leave their homes and were transported, at the beginning of winter, in open freight cars, to Russia. By the time they reached the Russian frontier, a quarter of them were already dead. The survivors were marched for six days toward Mogilev. Those who were in no condition to march were shot.

h. During the reoccupation of Bessarabia by German and other property being confiscated by the Hinka Guard. Preparations have been made to send the Jewish population into camps or ghettos near the Polish frontier between now and March 23. It is feared that they will be sent from there into Poland itself where they will suffer the same fate as the masses of Jews expelled from Romania.

5. It should be noted that among the Hungarian, Romanian and Slovakian Jews, there are several hundred families who are in possession of immigration visas for Palestine or some of the American countries. Above and beyond the steps that can be taken to secure general alleviation of the fate of persecuted and threatened Jewish populations, it is likewise a matter of great urgency to attempt approaches to the competent authorities, notably (for those emigrating to America) to the Italian Government with a view to obtaining transit visas or eventually, arranging specially organized convoys to enable the emigrants to reach their ports of embarkation.

> Richard Lichtheim
> Jewish Agency for Palestine
>   and
> Gerhart Riegner of the
>   World Jewish Congress
> Memorandum to
>   Archbishop Fillippo
>   Bernardini,
> the Nuncio in Switzerland
> March 18, 1942

High-Altitude Experiments at Dachau

Prisoners would go mad, and pull out their hair in an effort to relieve the pressure. They would tear their heads and face with their fingers and nails in an attempt to maim themselves in their madness. They would beat the walls with their hands and head, and scream in an effort to relieve pressure on their eardrums.

> Prisoner at Dachau
> March-August 1942

Testimony at war crimes trial, describing high altitude experiments conducted on inmates at the Dachau concentration camp. The experiments were conducted in decompression chambers, from which air was removed.

A Monsignor Sounds the Alarm

As I have already had the honor of informing Your Eminence, the Slovak government has decided to deport all the Jews; the operations involved commenced on the 25th and are being conducted in a most brutal manner. . . .

I have been told that during the [Slovak Council of State] session in which the deportation of the Jews was discussed, Bishop Vojtassak, instead of rising up against this inhuman project, had retained a totally passive attitude, limiting himself to objections of little importance. Afterwards, speaking with another bishop, he would have him understand that, according to his opinion, it would be better that ecclesiastical authorities remain out of the question, that it not create obstacles for the Government and for the President of the Republic, that the Jews are the worst enemies of Slovakia, that in any case things would have followed their course. . . .

More direct and, I would say, clear-sighted, is the position of His Excellency, Bishop Carsky, who, writing to a colleague on the necessity of taking a decisive attitude, concluded: "If we remain passive now when they are taking away the children of the Jews, what will we do when they take away the children of our people? . . .

I said above that the measures against the Jews are being carried out in the most brutal fashion. Concerning the treatment inflicted upon Jewish girls, from secure and controlled information it turns out that, after they are taken by force from their homes—(the raids, which began on the 25th and continue every night, are accomplished by the police and the militia of the Hlinka Guard)—they are concentrated in the locale in a building . . . which is located in the outskirts of Bratislava. There they are subjected to search, deprived of every object which they have taken along with them (suitcases, purses, rings, earrings, pens, foodstuffs, in sum everything, deprived of personal documents and assigned a simple registration number; if anyone protests . . . she is beaten. . . . They wait their turn to be loaded on to the cattle wagons that transport them to the German border. Several convoys have already departed. . . .

One is of the opinion that these poor girls are destined for prostitution or simply for massacre.

His Excellency Minister Sidor departs tomorrow for Rome, and I must leave incomplete the present report to make time to deliver it to him.

> Monsignor Giuseppe
>   Burzio, Charge d'Affairs
> Report to Luigi Cardinal
>   Maglione, Secretary of
>   State, the Vatican
> Bratislava
> March 31, 1942

APRIL 24, 1942

Jews in Germany may no longer use public transportation.

PROPAGANDA . . . AND MADNESS

Sassoons baboons, Rothschilds, etc. migrating to the United States and stinking up the whole country, in the wake of Zukor and the other fine flowers of Semite culture.

Look at Litvinov's face. The SOUL shining in beauty. Greek philosophy jettisoned, Justinian, jettisoned, the sense of LAW that built up all Europe, puked into the discard.

Sense of ENGLISH law, that was built up out of the Roman, puked into the discard. You will find out, brother, later or soon, and I should prefer it sooner, so as I should be able to meet some survivors.

Don't start a pogrom. That is, not an old style killing of small Jews.

> Ezra Pound
> Propaganda broadcast
> Rome
> April 30, 1942

From Ezra Pound Speaking, *edited by Leonard Doob.*

THE JEWS: "A WORLD QUESTION"

It is . . . not only a European problem! *The Jewish question is a world question!* Not only is Germany not safe in the face of the Jews as long as one Jew lives in Europe, but also the Jewish question is hardly solved in Europe so long as Jews live in the rest of the world.

> *Der Stuermer*
> May 7, 1942

Ley Calls for Extermination

It is not enough to isolate the Jewish enemy of mankind—the Jew has got to be exterminated.

> Robert Ley
> Speech
> Karlsruhe, Germany
> May 1942

Jewish Workers in Berlin

The Minister [Joseph Goebbels] says he has submitted to the Fuehrer a proposal for removing the Jews from Berlin. This has been opposed by economic authorities on the grounds that the Jews employed in the armaments industry are very much concerned with precision work and would be difficult to replace. It is now planned to hold five hundred leading Jews as hostages, to stand surety for the decent behavior of the Jews in Berlin.

> Propaganda Ministerial
> Conference
> Berlin
> May 1942

Cited in The Secret Conferences of Dr. Goebbels, *edited by Willi A. Boelcke.*

Problems with the Death Vans

TOP SECRET

The overhauling of vans by groups D and C is finished. While the vans of the first series can also be put into action if the weather is not too bad, the vans of the second series stop completely in rainy weather. If it has rained for instance for only one half hour, the van cannot be used because it simply skids away. It can only be used in absolutely dry weather. It is only a question now whether the van can only be used standing at the place of execution. First the van has to be brought to that place, which is possible only in good weather. The place of execution is 10 to 15 km away from the highways and is difficult of access because of its location; in damp or wet weather it is not accessible at all. If the persons to be executed are driven or led to that place, then they realize immediately what is going on and get restless, which is to be avoided as far as possible. There is only one way left; to load them at the collecting point and to drive them to the spot.

I ordered the vans of group D to be camouflaged as house trailers by putting one set of window shutters on each side of the small van and two on each side of the large vans, such as one often sees on farm houses in the country. The vans became so well-known, that not only the authorities but also the civilian population called the van "death van," as soon as one of these vehicles appeared. It is my opinion the van cannot be kept secret for any length of time, not even camouflaged. . . .

Because of the rough terrain and the indescribable road and highway conditions the caulking and rivets loosen in the course of time. I was asked if in such cases the vans should be brought to Berlin for repair. Transportation to Berlin would be much too expensive and would demand too much fuel. In order to save those expenses, I ordered them to have smaller leaks soldered and if that should no longer be possible, to notify Berlin immediately by radio, that Pol. Nre. is out of order. Besides that I ordered that during application of gas all the men were to be kept as far away from the vans as possible, so they should not suffer damage to their health by the gas which eventually would escape.

I should like to take this opportunity to bring the following to your attention: several commands have had the unloading after the application of gas done by their own men. I brought to the attention of the commanders of those S. K. concerned immense psychological injuries and damages to their health which that work can have for those men, even if not immediately, at least later on. The men complained to me about headaches which appeared after each unloading. Nevertheless they don't want to change the orders, because they are afraid prisoners called for that work could use an appropriate moment to flee. To protect the men from those damages, I request orders be issued accordingly.

The application of gas usually is not undertaken correctly. In order to come to an end as fast as possible, the driver presses the accelerator to the fullest extent. By doing that the persons to be executed suffer death from suffocation and not death by dozing off as was planned. My directions now have proved that by correct adjustment of the levers death comes faster and the prisoners fall asleep peacefully. Distorted faces and excretions, such as could be seen before, are no longer noticed.

Today I shall continue my journey to group B, where I can be reached with further news.

> Dr. August Becker
> Memorandum to SS
>   Obersturmbannfuehrer
>   Rauff
> Kiev
> May 16, 1942

SLAUGHTER AND REVENGE

Near a pit 20 by 20 meters long and three meters deep stood a table with bottles of cognac and food. At the table sits a German with an automatic gun in his hand. Frightened and despairing Jews are pushed into the pit naked, six at a time. . . . Between one sip of cognac and the next he shoots them. Among the 2,200 Jews the Germans shot that day were also my wife and my 13-year-old daughter.

. . . When the surviving Jews met in the synagogue to rend their garments and say Kaddish for the dead, a voice cried out in me: "not with prayers will you assuage our grief for the rivers of innocent blood that was spilled—but with revenge!" As soon as the Kaddish was over I banged the table and cried out: "Listen to me, unfortunate, death-condemned Jews! Know that sooner or later we are all doomed. But I shall not go like a sheep to the slaughter!"

Misha Gildenman
The Destruction of Koretz
Events of 1942

A Top Secret Request

On June 8, 1942, SS Sturmbannfuhrer Gunther . . . dressed in civilian clothes, walked into my office. . . . He ordered me to obtain for him, for a top secret mission, 100 kilos of prussic acid and to take it to a place known only to the truck driver. A few weeks later we set out for the potash plant near Kolin. . . .

We then set out with the truck for Lublin. SS Gruppenfuhrer Globocnik was waiting for us. He told us: "This is one of our most secret matters, indeed the most secret. Anyone who talks about it will be shot." . . .

Kurt Gerstein
Deposition to U.S. Army
April 26, 1945
Events of June-August 1942

From Le Monde Juif *XIX (January–March, 1964), trans. Rose Feitelson.*

JUNE 19, 1942

Jews in Germany can no longer own bicycles
or typewriters.

"A PLAN AND SCHEDULE"

The extermination is being executed according to a plan and schedule prepared in advance. Only a miracle can save us: the sudden end of the war. Otherwise, we are lost!

Emmanuel Ringelblum
Notes from the Warsaw Ghetto
June 25, 1942

WARSAW GHETTO EVACUATION ORDERED

All Jewish persons living in Warsaw, regardless of age and sex, will be resettled in the East. . . . *[Certain exclusions are noted.]* . . . Every Jew being resettled may take 15kg. of his property as baggage. All valuables such as gold, jewelry, money, etc., may be taken. Food is to be taken for three days.

Decree
Issued through the Judenrat
July 22, 1942

A POLISH WITNESS AT TREBLINKA

Does he remember the first convoy of Jews from Warsaw on July 22, 1942?

He recalls the first convoy very well, and when all those Jews were brought here, people wondered, "What's to be done with them?" Clearly, they'd be killed, but no one yet knew how. When people began to understand what was happening, they were appalled, and they commented privately that since the world began, no one had ever murdered so many people that way.

They worked their fields?
Certainly they worked, but not as willingly as usual. They had to work, but when they saw all this, they thought: "Our house may be surrounded. We may be arrested too!"

Were they afraid for the Jews too?
Well, he says, it's this way: if I cut my finger, it doesn't hurt him. They knew about the Jews; the convoys came in here, and then went to the camp, and the people vanished.

> Czeslaw Borowi
> Interviewed in *Shoah: An
> Oral History of the
> Holocaust* by Claude
> Lanzmann
> Treblinka
> Citing events of July 22, 1942
> and thereafter

SEEKING PAPAL HELP

In recent reports to the Department . . . I have called attention to the opinion that the failure of the Holy See to protest publicly against Nazi atrocities is endangering its moral prestige and is undermining faith both in the church and in the Holy Father himself. I have on a number of occasions informally reminded the Vatican of this danger and so have certain of my colleagues but without result. The answer is invariably that the Pope in his speeches has already condemned offenses against morality in wartime and that to be specific now would only make matters worse.

> Harold H. Tittmann
> Telegram to the U.S.
>   Secretary of State,
> via U.S. Minister in
>   Switzerland
> July 30, 1942

POSTED AT TREBLINKA

Jews of Warsaw, Attention!

You are in a transit camp from which you will be sent to a labor camp. In order to avoid epidemics, you must present your clothing and belongings for immediate disinfection. Gold, money, foreign currency, and jewelry should be deposited with the cashiers in return for a receipt. They will be returned to you later when you present the receipt. Bodily cleanliness requires that everyone bathe before continuing the journey.

> Sign in Polish and German
> Treblinka
> Summer 1942

Cited in Belzec, Sobibor, Treblinka *by Yitzhak Arad.*

THE RAVENSBRUCK "RABBITS"

Medical experiments on women prisoners begin at Ravensbruck. Experiments on these "rabbits" (human guinea pigs) will include operations involving bones, muscles, and nerves; amputation of limbs; sterilization by various means; and the simulation of battlefield wounds.

August 1, 1942

Cited at the war crimes trials.

Last Diary Entry

I am watering the flowers. My bald head in the window. What a splendid target.

He [the guard] has a rifle. Why is he standing and looking on calmly?

He has no orders to shoot.

And perhaps he was a village teacher in civilian life, or a notary, a street sweeper in Leipzig, a waiter in Cologne?

What would he do if I nodded to him? Waved my hand in a friendly gesture?

Perhaps he doesn't know that things are—as they are?

He may have arrived only yesterday, from far away. . . .

Janusz Korczak
Ghetto Diary
Warsaw ghetto
August 4, 1942

The following day, Korczak, his entire staff, and the 200 Jewish children in his orphanage were shipped off to Treblinka.

A Plan for Wholesale Extermination

Transmitting Memorandum of Conversation with Secretary of Jewish Congress, Geneva, concerning Report that Germans are Considering Wholesale Extermination of Jews.

At the suggestion of the Legation at Bern, I have the honor to enclose a copy of a memorandum on the above. . . .

I desire to reiterate my belief in the utter seriousness of my informant.

(From the memorandum enclosed):

This morning Mr. Gerhart M. Riegner, Secretary of the World Jewish Congress in Geneva, called in great agitation. He stated that he had just received a report from a German business man of considerable prominence, who is said to have excellent political and military connections in Germany . . . to the effect that there has been and is being considered in Hitler's headquarters a plan to exterminate all Jews from Germany and German controlled areas in Europe after they have been concentrated in the east (presumably Poland). The number involved is said to be between three-and-a-half to four million and the object is to permanently settle the Jewish question in Europe. The mass execution if decided upon would allegedly take place this fall.

Riegner stated that according to his informant . . . prussic acid was mentioned as a means of accomplishing the executions.

> Howard Elting, Jr.
> American Vice Consul in
>   Geneva
> Memorandum to the U.S.
>   Secretary of State
> August 10, 1942

PRIDE IN HIS WORK

[A Nazi official] asked me, "But wouldn't it be wiser to cremate the corpses instead of burying them? Another generation may perhaps judge these things differently!" I replied: "Gentlemen, if there were ever, after us, a generation cowardly and so soft that they could not understand our work which is so good, so necessary, then, gentlemen, all of National Socialism will have been in vain. We ought, on the contrary, to bury bronze tablets stating that it was we who had the courage to carry out this gigantic task!"

> Odilo Globocnik
> Belzec
> August 15, 1942

Cited in The Holocaust Reader, *edited by Lucy Dawidowicz.*

Train from Lvov

A few minutes [after 7 A.M.] a train arrived [at Belzec] from Lvov, with 45 cars holding 6,700 people, of whom 1,450 were already dead on arrival. . . . Wirth [commandant of the Belzec camp] and I were standing on the ramp in front of the death chambers. Completely nude men, women, young girls, children, babies, cripples, filed by. At the corner stood a heavy SS man, who told the poor people, in a pastoral voice: "No harm will come to you. You just have to breathe very deeply, that strengthens the lungs . . ."

. . . The people wait inside the gas chambers. . . . In vain. They can be heard weeping. "like in the synagogue," says Professor Pfannenstiel, his eyes glued to a window in the wood door.

> Kurt Gerstein
> Deposition to U.S. Army
> April 26, 1945
> Events of August 20, 1942

From Le Monde Juif *XIX (January–March, 1964), trans. Rose Feitelson.*

PERCEPTION

A rather wild story.

> British Foreign Office view
> of report that Nazis
> planned to kill all
> European Jews
> August 1942

Cited in Britain and the Jews of Europe 1939–1945 *by Bernard Wasserstein.*

A REFUSAL AND A SUICIDE

An order for the deportation of Jews from the Warsaw Ghetto was issued recently, and daily about seven thousand were being removed to "an unknown destination." There seems to be reason for believing that these deportees are being killed before they reach any destination. The Chairman of the Council of the Warsaw Ghetto, Engineer Cherniakow, whom the Gestapo tried to compel to prepare the daily lists of the people to be removed from the ghetto, refused to give them those lists and took his own life rather than comply.

> Joint Foreign Committee of
> the Board of Deputies
> and the Anglo-Jewish
> Association
> London
> July–August 1942 report

EVALUATION BY WELLES

He [Under-Secretary of State Sumner Welles] seems to think that the real purpose of the Nazi government is to use Jews in connection with war work both in Nazi Germany and in Nazi Poland and Russia.

Rabbi Stephen Wise
Letter to Supreme Court
Justice Frankfurter
September 4, 1942

WHO IS FIT TO LIVE?

With regard to the destruction of asocial life, Dr. Goebbels is of the opinion that the following groups should be exterminated: Jews and gypsies, unconditionally, Poles who have to serve 3–4 years of penal servitude, and Czechs and Germans who are sentenced to death or penal servitude for life or to security custody for life. The idea of exterminating them by labor is the best. For the rest however, except in the aforementioned cases, every case has to be dealt with individually.

Discussion in Berlin
September 14, 1942

Introduced into evidence at Nuremburg.

THE JEWS AND VIENNA

Every Jew who exerts influence in Europe is a danger to European culture. If anyone reproaches me with having driven from this city—which was once the European metropolis of Jewry—tens of thousands upon tens of thousands of Jews into the ghetto of the East, I feel myself compelled to reply: I see in this an action contributing to European culture.

> Baldur von Schirach
> Speech
> European Youth Congress
> Vienna, Austria
> September 4, 1942

Penalty for Harboring Jews

Any Pole, who during and after the resettlement, harbors or hides a Jew, will be shot.

> Dr. Pernutz, Tarnow District
>   Prefect
> Proclamation
> September 15, 1942

Food Rations Restricted

Jews [in Germany] will no longer receive the following foods [on their food ration cards], beginning with the 42nd distribution period (19 October 1942): meat, meat products, eggs, wheat products (cake, white bread, wheat rolls, wheat flour, etc.), whole milk, fresh skimmed milk, as well as such food distributed not on food ration cards issued uniformly throughout the Reich but on local supply certificates or by special announcement of the nutrition office on extra coupons of the food cards.

> German Ministry of
>   Agriculture
> Directive
> September 18, 1942

QUESTIONS FOR THE POPE

The following was received from the Geneva Office of the Jewish Agency for Palestine in a letter dated August 30th, 1942. That office received the report from two reliable eye-witnesses (Aryans). . . .

(1) Liquidation of the Warsaw Ghetto is taking place. Without any distinction all Jews, irrespective of age or sex, are being removed from the Ghetto in groups and shot. . . .

(2) These mass executions take place, not in Warsaw, but in especially prepared camps for the purpose. . . .

(3) Jews deported from Germany, Belgium, Holland, France, and Slovakia are sent to be butchered. . . .

(4) Inasmuch as butcherings of this kind would attract great attention in the West, they must first of all deport them to the East, where less opportunity is afforded to outsiders of knowing what is going on. . . . A great number of the German refugees were taken to Theresienstadt. This place, however, is only an interim station and the people there await the same fate.

(5) Arrangements are made for new deportations as soon as space is made by executions. Caravans of such deportees being transported in cattle cars are often seen. . . .

I should much appreciate it if Your Eminence could inform me whether the Vatican has any information that would tend to confirm the reports contained in this memorandum. If so, I should like to know whether the Holy Father has any suggestions as to any practical manner in which the forces of civilized public opinion could be utilized in order to prevent a continuation of these barbarities.

> Myron Taylor
> Memorandum to Vatican
>   Secretary of State Cardinal
>   Maglione*
> September 26, 1942.

---

*Because of their respective positions, the memo was actually from President Roosevelt to Pope Pius XII.

FEAR OF SLAUGHTER

It is feared that the Nazis may be resorting to wholesale slaughter, preferring to kill all Jews rather than use their labor.

National Jewish Monthly
October 1942

EXPANSION AT TREBLINKA

In March 1942, the Germans began to erect another camp, Treblinka B, in the neighborhood of Treblinka A, intended to become a place of torment for Jews.

The erection of this camp was closely connected with the German plans aiming at a complete destruction of the Jewish population in Poland which necessitated that creation of a machinery by means of which the Polish Jews could be killed in numbers. Late in April 1942, the erection of the first three chambers was finished in which these general massacres were to be performed by means of steam. Somewhat later the creation of the real death building was finished, which contained ten death chambers. It was opened for wholesale murders early in autumn 1942. . . .

After unloading in the [railroad] siding all victims were assembled in one place where men were separated from women and children. In the first days of the existence of the camp the victims were made to believe that after a short stay in the camp, necessary for bathing and disinfection, they would be sent farther east, for work. Explanations of this sort were given by SS men who assisted at the unloading of the transports and further explanations could be read in notices stuck on the walls of barracks. But later, when more transports had to be dealt with, the Germans dropped all pretenses and only tried to accelerate the procedure.

All victims had to strip off their clothes and shoes, which

were collected afterwards, whereupon all victims, women and children first, were driven into the death chambers. Those too slow or too weak to move quickly were driven on by rifle butts, by whipping and kicking. . . . Many slipped and fell, the next victims pressed forward and stumbled over them. Small children were simply thrown inside. After being filled up to capacity the chambers were hermetically closed and steam was let in. In a few minutes, all was over. The Jewish menial workers had to remove bodies from the platform and to bury them in mass graves. By and by, as new transports arrived, the cemetery grew, extending in eastern direction.

> Polish Government
> Commission
> Report on the Investigation
> of German Crimes in
> Poland
> Events of 1942

Cited at the Nuremburg War Crimes Trial, 1945.

EYEWITNESS ACCOUNT

Without screaming or weeping, these people undressed, stood around in family groups, kissed each other, said farewells and waited. . . . I watched a family of about eight persons, a man and woman, both about 50, with their children of about one, eight, ten, and two grown-up daughters of about 20 and 24. An old woman with snow white hair was holding the one-year-old child in her arms and singing to it and tickling it. The child was cooing with delight. The couple were looking on with tears in their eyes. . . .

I found myself confronted by a tremendous grave. People were closely wedged together and lying on top of each other so that only their heads were visible. Nearly all had blood running over their shoulders from their heads. Some of the people shot were still moving. . . . The people, completely naked, went down the steps which were cut in the clay wall pit and clambered over the heads of the people lying there, to the place where the SS man directed them. They lay down in front of the dead or injured people, some caressed those who were still alive and spoke to them in a low voice. Then I heard a series of shots.

> Hermann Graebe*
> Dubno ghetto vicinity,
>   Ukraine
> October 5, 1942

REPORT FROM LODZ

In Lodz thousands of Jewish families are taken away from the ghetto systematically and nobody ever hears from them again. They are poisoned by gas.

> Jewish Telegraphic Agency
> October 6, 1942

RESPONSE FROM THE VATICAN

Holy See replied today [October 10] to Mr. Taylor's letter regarding treatment of the Jews in Poland in an informal and unsigned statement handed me by the Cardinal Secretary of

---

*Sworn affidavit read to the International Military Tribunal, Nuremberg, November 10, 1945.

State. After thanking Ambassador Taylor for bringing the matter to the attention of the Holy See the statement says that reports of severe measures taken against non-Aryans have also reached the Holy See from other sources but that up to the present time it has not been possible to verify the accuracy thereof. However, the statement adds it is well known that the Holy See is taking advantage of every opportunity offered in order to mitigate the suffering of non-Aryans.

I regret that Holy See could not have been more helpful but it was evident from the attitude of the Cardinal that it has no practical suggestions to make. I think it is perhaps likely that the belief is held that there is little hope of checking Nazi barbarities by any method except that of physical force coming from without.

> Harold H. Tittmann
> Telegram to U.S. Secretary of
> State
> via the U.S. Minister in
> Switzerland
> October 16, 1942

French Underground Paper Reports

The Boche torturers are burning and asphyxiating thousands of men, women, and children deported from France.

> J'Accuse
> French underground
> newspaper
> October 20, 1942

Unique in History

In the occupied countries of Europe a policy is now being put into effect, whose avowed object is the extermination of a whole people. It is a policy of systematic murder of innocent civilians which in its dimensions, its ferocity and its organization is unique in the history of mankind.

Jewish Frontier
November 1942

NOVEMBER 7, 1942

Allies invade North Africa.

MEDICAL CONFERENCE PROGRAM

Theme: "Problems Arising from Hardships of Sea and Winter."
Papers include: "Prevention and Treatment of Freezing,"
and "Warming up after Freezing to the Danger Point."

German medical conference
1942

Conference heard papers on work at Dachau, where inmates were deliberately frozen in experiments. Cited at war crimes trials.

DECEMBER 2, 1942

Day of Mourning and Prayer on behalf of
European Jewry. The United States and 29
foreign countries join in the commemoration.

ACTION . . . OR DOOM?

Unless action is taken immediately, the Jews of Hitler Europe are doomed.

> Jewish leaders Rabbi
>   Stephen Wise, Henry
>   Monsky, Rabbi Israel
>   Rosenberg, Maurice
>   Wertheim, and Adolph
>   Held
> Meeting with President
>   Roosevelt
> December 8, 1942

JEWS IN NORTH AFRICA

Last night we had a two-ring conference after dinner. . . . Murphy and Holmes had been sent by Ike [General Eisenhower] to perk up Darlan [French government leader in North Africa following the Allied invasion] on his liberalization of Nazi-inspired decrees in the form of a new ordinance, which is supposedly being rewritten. Darlan had shown Murphy and Holmes a letter from a rabbi in Constantine, urging that reform of the hard and unjust laws against the Jews in Africa be modified slowly.

> Harry C. Butcher
> Diary excerpt
> Algiers
> December 10, 1942

Cited in My Three Years with Eisenhower, *1946.*

HEADLINE FROM THE JEWISH CHRONICLE

TWO MILLION JEWS SLAUGHTERED:
MOST TERRIBLE MASSACRE OF ALL TIME:
APPALLING HORRORS OF NAZI MASS MURDERS

Headline
The Jewish Chronicle
London
December 11, 1942

THE DELICATE ISSUE OF ATROCITIES

British propaganda is taken up so much with the alleged anti-Jewish atrocities in the East that the Minister [Joseph Goebbels] believes the time has now come to do something about this propaganda campaign. The subject, of course, is rather delicate, and we had best not engage in polemics but instead give particular prominence to British atrocities in India, in Iran and in Egypt. Our best weapon against this propaganda campaign is an offensive, and for that the British are providing us with enough material. The atrocity stories, however, must be presented by us on a stronger note and must be vigorously supported by the German press so that they really make an impact in the world.

Propaganda Ministerial
Conference
Berlin
December 12, 1942

Cited in The Secret Conferences of Dr. Goebbels, *edited by Willi A. Boelcke.*

How to Make Soap, Nazi Style

I boiled the soap out of the bones of women and men. The process of boiling alone took several days—from 3 to 7. During two manufacturing processes, in which I directly participated, more than 25 kilograms of soap were produced. The amount of human fat necessary for these two processes was 70 to 80 kilograms collected from some 40 bodies.

> Sigmund Mazur
> Danzig Anatomic Institute
> Testimony presented at
>   war crimes trial
> Events of early 1940s

945 Polish Jewish Communities Vanish

By the end of 1942, Jews in the General Government of Poland had been crowded into 55 localities, whereas before the German invasion there had been approximately 1,000 Jewish settlements within the same area.

> Reported in the Official
>   Gazette for the General
>   Government
> January 1943

Learning Arabic

I have already written that I've begun to learn Arabic. It must be understood that I am not learning this language simply because I like it. I began—and I want very much to complete it—to learn this language because a large portion of the inhabitants of Eretz Yisrael and its neighbors speak this tongue. And in order to fulfill my goal [to be a diplomat in Israel] it is necessary for me to at least learn to speak the language.

Moses Flinker
Diary excerpt
Brussels, Belgium
Early 1940s

From The Lad Moses: The Diary of Moses Flinker.

The Disbelievers

Nearly 30 percent of those asked dismissed the news that 2 million Jews had been killed in Europe as just a rumor. Another 24 percent had no opinion on the question.

Gallup poll
January 1943

From Beyond Belief *by Deborah E. Lipstadt.*

On Jewish Politics

Jews must always battle Jews. It's the only politics open to a stateless people. The only victories they can hope to enjoy are victories over each other.

Peter Bergson
Comment
New York City
January 1943

Commenting on a failed attempt to unify 33 Jewish organizations in the support of a pageant on behalf of European Jewry threatened with extinction.

Cited in A Child of the Century *by Ben Hecht, 1954.*

ON FLEEING EUROPE

The story of our struggle has finally become known. We lost our home, which means the familiarity of daily life. We lost our occupation, which means the confidence that we are in some use in the world. We lost our language, which means the naturalness of reactions, the simplicity of gestures, the unaffected expression of feelings. We left our relatives in the Polish ghettos and our best friends have been killed in concentration camps, and that means the rupture of our private lives.

> Hannah Arendt
> Article
> *The Menorah Journal*
> January 1943

HIMMLER SEEKS MORE TRAINS

I need your support. If I am to wind things up quickly, I must have trains for transports.

> Heinrich Himmler
> Letter to the Reich Minister
>   of Transport
> January 20, 1943

A CALL FOR RESISTANCE

On January 22, 1943, six months will have passed since the deportations from Warsaw began. We all remember well the days of terror during which 300,000 of our brothers and sisters were cruelly put to death in the death camp of Treblinka. . . . The blood-stained murderers have a particular aim . . . to reassure the Jewish population in order that the next deportation can be carried out without difficulty, with a minimum of forces and without losses to the Germans. . . .

You must be prepared to resist, not to give yourselves up like sheep to slaughter. Not even one Jew must go to the [deportation] train. . . . Let everyone be ready to die like a man!

> Jewish Fighting Organization
> Appeal
> January 1943

BRITISH FOREIGN OFFICE WORRIES ABOUT EMBARRASSMENT

There is a possibility that the Germans or their satellites may change over from the policy of extermination to one of extrusion, and aim as they did before the war at embarrassing other countries by flooding them with alien immigrants.

> British Foreign Office
> Memorandum to U.S. State
> Department
> January 20, 1943

PROCLAMATION ATTACKS JEWS ANEW

The conspiracy of international capitalism and Bolshevism is at the same time by no means a contradictory phenomenon, but a natural occurrence as the impelling force in both is that race which, in its hatred, for thousands of years has repeatedly butchered mankind, torn it asunder inwardly, plundered it economically, and destroyed it politically. International Jewry is the ferment of the decomposition of peoples and States. It is so today, just as it was in antiquity; and it will remain so until the nations find strength to rid themselves of this source of disease.

> Adolf Hitler
> Proclamation
> January 30, 1943

A Cry for American Support

American Jewry has not done—and has made no effort to do—its elementary duty toward the millions of Jews who are captive and doomed to die in Europe. . . . The chief organizations of American Jewry . . . in this dire hour, unequalled even in Jewish history [do not] unite for the purpose of seeking ways to forestall the misfortune or at least to reduce its scope; to save those who *perhaps* can still be saved. . . . What has such rescue work to do with political differences?

> Hayim Greenberg
> "Bankrupt," in *Yiddisher Kemfer*
> February 12, 1943

A Business Deal

To the Central Construction Office of the SS and Police, Auschwitz:

Subject: Crematoria 2 and 3 for the camp.

We acknowledge receipt of your order for five triple furnaces, including two electric elevators for raising the corpses and one emergency elevator. A practical installation for stoking coal was also ordered and one for transporting ashes.

> I. A. Topf and Sons
> Letter
> Erfurt
> February 12, 1943

SHE HAD NO CHOICE

One morning, on my way to school, I passed by a small Jewish children's home [in Amsterdam]. The Germans were loading the children, who ranged in age from babies to eight-year-olds, on trucks. They were upset, and crying. When they did not move fast enough the Nazis picked them up, by an arm, a leg, the hair, and threw them into the trucks. . . . That was the moment I decided that if there was anything I could do to thwart such atrocities, I would do it. . . .

   I . . . moved out into part of a large house . . . about twenty miles east of Amsterdam [to hide a Jewish family]. . . . Overnight . . . four Germans, accompanied by a Dutch Nazi policeman, came and searched the house. They did not find the hiding place . . . had learned from experience that sometimes it paid to go. . . . Later the Dutch policeman came back alone. I had a small revolver . . . I felt I had no choice except to kill him. I would do it again, under the same circumstances, but it still bothers me. . . .

> Marion Pritchard
> Amsterdam and vicinity
> Events of 1943–45

Cited in The Courage to Care, *edited by Carol Rittner and Sondra Myers, 1986.*

GHETTO ORDERED DESTROYED

For reasons of security I herewith order that the Warsaw Ghetto be pulled down after the concentration camp has been moved. . . . An overall plan for the razing of the ghetto is to be submitted to me. In any case we must achieve the disappearance from sight of the living space for 500,000 sub-humans that has existed up to now, but could never be suitable for Germans.

> Heinrich Himmler
> Order
> February 16, 1943

FOR SALE TO HUMANITY: 70,000 JEWS

Guaranteed Human Beings at $50 apiece.

> Committee for a Jewish Army
> Ad
> *The New York Times*
> February 16, 1943

Ad was an attempt to stir up interest in reports that the Rumanian government was willing to release its Jews at a rate of about $50 each.

STATE DEPARTMENT VIEWS THE REFUGEE PROBLEM

The refugee problem should not be considered as being confined to persons of any particular race or faith.

> U.S. State Department
> Memorandum to British
> Foreign Office
> February 25, 1943

A Plea for Sanctuary

Two million Jews have already been exterminated. The world can no longer plead that the ghastly facts are unknown and unconfirmed. At this moment expressions of sympathy, without accompanying attempts to launch acts of rescue, become a hollow mockery in the ears of the dying.

The democracies have a clear duty before them. Let them negotiate with Germany through the neutral countries concerning the possible release of the Jews in the occupied countries. Let havens be designated in the vast territories of the United Nations which will give sanctuary to those fleeing from imminent murder. Let the gates of Palestine be opened to all who can reach the shores of the Jewish homeland. The Jewish community of Palestine will welcome with joy and thanksgiving all delivered from Nazi hands.

> Chaim Weizmann
> Speech
> March 1, 1943

The Fuehrer is Happy

The Fuehrer is happy to hear from me that most of the Jews have now been evacuated from Berlin. The Jews will certainly be the losers in this war—one way or the other.

> Joseph Goebbels
> Statement at propaganda
>   Ministerial Conference
> Berlin
> March 2, 1943

JEWISH UNDERGROUND EXECUTIONS

The execution [of Jewish underground members] took place on March 4, 1943. It was announced publicly on placards that were posted throughout Berlin. The names of the condemned were given in usual Nazi fashion. The men were referred to as Israel and the women as Sarah. Thus the Hitler regime sought to suggest to the German population that only Jews were resistance fighters. Similar trials and verdicts against German anti-Fascists were, as a rule, not announced. . . .

The [total] number [in the Baum group] decapitated was 22. Eighteen were Jewish anti-Fascists, three German anti-Fascists, and one French woman. Nine Jewish activists of the Baum group perished in concentration camps. [The Nazis reported that Herbert Baum committed suicide. It is believed more likely that he died under torture.]

Ber Mark
Bleter Far Geszichte
Vol. XIV, 1961
Events of 1943–44

Cited in "The Herbert Baum Group: Jewish Resistance in Germany in the Years 1937–1942," in They Fought Back, *edited and translated by Yuri Suhl.*

PRAYER FROM A PAGEANT

Almighty God, Father of the poor and weak, Hope of all who dream of goodness and justice; Almighty God who favored the children of Israel with His light—we are here to affirm that this light still shines in us.

We are here to say our prayers for the two million who have been killed in Europe, because they bear the name of your first children—the Jews. . . .

We are here to affirm that the innocence of their lives and

the dream of goodness in their souls are witnesses that will never be silent. They shall never die.

> Ben Hecht
> From pageant
> *We Will Never Die*
> Madison Square Garden,
>   New York City
> March 9, 1943

WARSAW GHETTO UPRISING

Hardly had operation [to deport all remaining Jews from the ghetto], than we ran into strong concerted fire by the Jews and bandits. The tank and two armored cars pelted with Molotov cocktails. . . . Owing to this enemy counterattack we had to withdraw.

> General Juergen Stroop
> Report to superiors in Berlin
> Warsaw
> April 19, 1943

NEWS HEADLINES ON THE BERMUDA CONFERENCE

REFUGEE CONFERENCE DELEGATE WARNS OF FALSE HOPES FOR AID

> *Denver Post*
> Page 3
> April 19, 1943

REFUGEES ARE WARNED TO WAIT

> *Seattle Times*
> Page 3
> April 19, 1943

CONFERENCE SAYS LARGE SCALE RESCUE NOT POS-
SIBLE NOW

San Francisco Examiner
Page 11
April 22, 1943

BERMUDA PARLEY DECIDES MOST PLANS UNFEASIBLE

Chicago Tribune
Page 9
April 23, 1943

SCANT HOPE SEEN FOR AXIS VICTIMS

The New York Times
Page 19
April 25, 1943

REFUGEE REMOVAL CALLED IMPOSSIBLE

Washington Post
Page 1
April 30, 1943

Cited in The Abandonment of the Jews, *by David S. Wyman.*

BERMUDA CONFERENCE CRITICISM

No Jewish organizations are represented [at the Bermuda
conference on refugees] and the conference is purely explor-
atory, can make no decisions and must submit whatever
recommendations it may have to the executive committee of
the Intergovernmental Committee on Refugees. Meanwhile the
hourly slaughter of the Jews goes on.

New Republic
April 26, 1943

BERMUDA CONFERENCE COMMUNIQUE

The United States and United Kingdom delegates examined the refugee problem in all its aspects including the position on those potential refugees who are still in the grip of the Axis powers without any immediate prospect of escape. Nothing was excluded from their analysis and everything that held out any possibility, however remote, of a solution of the problem was carefully investigated and thoroughly discussed. From the outset it was realized that any recommendation that the delegates could make to their governments must pass two tests: Would any recommendation submitted interfere with or delay the war effort of the United Nations and was the recommendation capable of accomplishment under war conditions? The delegates at Bermuda felt bound to reject certain proposals which were not capable of meeting these tests. The delegates were able to agree on a number of concrete recommendations which they are jointly submitting to their governments and which, it is felt, will pass the tests set forth above and will lead to the relief of a substantial number of refugees of all races and nationalities. Since the recommendations necessarily concern governments other than those represented at the Bermuda conference and involve military considerations, they must remain confidential. It may be said, however, that in the course of discussion the refugee problem was broken down into its main elements. Questions of shipping, food, and supply were fully investigated. The delegates also agreed on recommendations regarding the form of intergovernmental organization which was best fitted, in their opinion, to handle the problem in the future. This organization would have to be flexible enough to permit it to consider without prejudice any new factors that might come to its attention. In each of these fields the delegates were able to submit agreed proposals for consideration of their respective governments.

U.S. and British delegations
Communique
Bermuda
April 30, 1943

THE SENATOR SOUNDS A WARNING

Two million Jews in Europe have been killed off already and another five million Jews are awaiting the same fate unless they are saved immediately. Every day, every hour, every minute that passes, thousands of them are being exterminated. . . . [Unless we act we face] the moral responsibility of being passive bystanders.

> William Langer
> Speech
> U.S. Senate
> Washington D.C.
> May 1943

GHETTO FIGHTING RAGES ON

[When Jews fought back, the Nazis decided to burn down every building in the Warsaw ghetto.]

The Jews stayed in the burning buildings until because of the fear of getting burned alive they jumped down from the upper stories. . . . With their bones broken, they still tried to crawl across the street into buildings which had not yet been set on fire. . . . Despite the danger of being burned alive the Jews and bandits often preferred to return into the flames rather than risk being caught by us.

> General Juergen Stroop
> Report to superiors in
>   Berlin
> Warsaw
> May 1943

COMMENT ON THE BERMUDA CONFERENCE

A mockery and a cruel jest . . . [on the] wretched, doomed victims of Hitler's tyranny.

> Committee for a Jewish Army
> Advertisement
> *The New York Times*
> May 4, 1943

THE WORLD WENT ON

As flames rose all around the [Warsaw] ghetto, the Poles outside went about their lives as usual. I remember the children riding on the merry-go-round. This is the one impression I shall always remember. During this great battle for freedom, the world stood silently—or went on as usual. We begged for guns, for ammunition, for planes, for even a symbol of world support. We knew we couldn't win. We wanted only to die with dignity. The world did . . . nothing.

> Vladka Meed
> Interview in *Our Age*
> April 21, 1963, Volume 4,
>   No. 13
> Events of May 1943

EXCERPTS FROM A SUICIDE NOTE

By my death I wish to give expression to my most profound protest against the inaction in which the world watches and permits the destruction of the Jewish people.

I know that there is no great value to the life of a man, especially today. But since I did not succeed in achieving it in my lifetime, perhaps I shall be able by my death to contribute to the arousing from lethargy of those who could and must act in order that even now, perhaps at the last moment, the handful of Polish Jews who are still alive can be saved from certain destruction.

My life belongs to the Jewish people of Poland, and therefore I hand it over to them now.

> Szmul Zygielbojm
> Letter
> May 11, 1943

FINAL BATTLE REPORT

The former Jewish quarter of Warsaw is no longer in existence.

> General Juergen Stroop
> Report to superiors in
>   Berlin
> Warsaw
> May 16, 1943

TAKING STEPS TO GUARD THE GOLD

On April 13, 1943 the former German dentist Ernst Israel Tichauer and his wife, Ellen Sara Tichauer, nee Rosenthal, were committed to the court prison by the Security Service. Since that time all German and Russian Jews who were turned over to us had their golden bridgework, crowns, and fillings pulled or broken out. This happens always one to two hours before the respective action.

Since 13 April 1943, 516 German and Russian Jews have been finished off. On the basis of a definite investigation gold was taken only in two actions on 14 April 1943 from 172, and on 27 April 1943 from 164 Jews. About fifty percent of the Jews had gold teeth, bridgework, or fillings. Hauptscharfuehrer Rube of the Security Service was always personally present and he took the gold along.

Before 13 April 1943 this was not done.

> Warden Gunther
> Letter to General
>   Commissioner of White
>   Ruthenia
> Minsk Prison
> May 31, 1943

SHIPWRECK

We left Piraeus [bound, illegally, for Palestine] at around eleven o'clock at night. At two in the morning the captain was at our door. He said, "Young men, our boat is sinking. I want no panic. If anybody panics I will shoot him. So please be calm. . . . When I say jump, you will jump." There were no life jackets, no lifeboats. We had no radio. At first we thought he was joking, but soon we could feel that something was very wrong with the boat, and before we knew it we were in the water . . . with only heaven above us and water beneath.

> Herman Herskocic
> In *Voices from the Holocaust*
> Edited by Sylvia Rothchild
> Events of 1943

A Meeting with Klaus Barbie

[Klaus Barbie was] a smiling man. At first I found him very, very charming. He was dressed in light grey, carrying a cat which was a darker shade of grey. He came towards us very nicely, stroking the cat. First he looked at my father, then my mother, and then came to me and said I was very pretty. Still stroking the cat, he put it gently on the table and asked my mother where her other children had gone. We really didn't know. They'd gone into hiding in the country two days before and we didn't have their address. Slowly, he came up to me and took hold of my long hair, rolling it gently along his hand. When he reached my skull, he yanked it as hard as he could and repeated his questions over and over again. He slapped me and knocked me onto the floor and picked me up with the end of his foot. . . . [Simone was then separated from her parents.]

He knocked me about all day. My face was completely torn to pieces. My lip was split. I was covered in blood, and I hadn't eaten. He took me to my mother's cell. He had the door opened and called to my mother. "Well, there you are, you can be proud of yourself." The beating continued for five days.

> Simone Legrange
> Age 13
> Montluc prison, France
> Recalling events of June 6,
>   1943

Testimony at Barbie's war crimes trial. Cited in Klaus Barbie: The Butcher of Lyons *by Tom Bower.*

No Way to Run a Genocide

The fact that Jews receive special treatment [i.e., are murdered] requires no further discussion. However, it appears hardly believable that this is done in the way described in the report of the General Commissioner of 1 June 1943. . . .

Imagine only that these occurrences would become known to the other side and exploited by them! Most likely such propaganda would have no effect only because people who heard and read about it simply would not be ready to believe it.

To lock men, women, and children into barns and to set fire to them does not appear to be a suitable method of combatting bands, even if it is desired to exterminate the population. This method is not worthy of the German cause and hurts our reputation severely.

Secret report from Kube to
Alfred Rosenberg
June 18, 1943

A POLICE REPORT FROM POLAND

Solution of Jewish Question in Galicia

Nothing but catastrophical conditions were found in the ghettos of Rawa-Ruska and Rohatyn. . . .

The Jews of Rawa-Ruska, fearing the evacuation, had concealed those suffering from spotted fever in underground holes. When evacuation was to start, the police found that 3,000 Jews suffering from spotted fever lay about in this ghetto. In order to destroy this center of pestilence at once, every police officer inoculated against spotted fever was called into action. Thus we succeeded to destroy this plague-boil, losing thereby only one officer. Almost the same conditions were found in Rohatyn. . . .

Since we received more and more alarming reports on the Jews becoming armed in an ever increasing manner, we started during the last fortnight . . . an action throughout the whole of the district of Galicia with the intent to use strongest measures to destroy the Jewish gangsterdom. Special measures were found necessary during the action to dissolve the ghetto in Lwow where the dug-out mentioned above had been established. Here we had to act brutally from the beginning, in order to avoid losses on our side; we had to blow up, or to burn down, several houses. On this occasion, the surprising fact arose that we were able to catch about 20,000 Jews instead of 12,000 Jews who had registered. We had to pull at least 3,000 Jewish corpses out of every kind of hiding places; they had committed suicide by taking poison. . . .

Despite the extraordinary burden heaped upon every single SS-Police officer during these actions, mood and spirit of the men were extraordinarily good and praiseworthy from the first to the last day. . . .

Together with the evacuation action, we executed the confiscation of Jewish property. Very high amounts were confiscated and paid over to the Special Staff "Reinhard." Apart from furniture and many textile goods, the following amounts were confiscated and turned over to Special Staff "Reinhard":

20.952   kilograms of gold wedding rings.
   7   Stamp collections, complete.
   1   Suitcase with pocket knives.
   1   basket of fountain pens and propelled pencils.
   3   bags filled with rings—not genuine.
  35   wagons of furs.
  73   kilograms of gold teeth and inlays.

> Lt. General of Police
> Katzmann
> To Krueger, General of
> Police
> East Galicia, Poland
> June 20, 1943

A QUESTION FOR THE PRESIDENT

What About the Jews, FDR?

> Max Lerner
> Editorial
> *PM*
> July 22, 1943

GAS BEFORE REMOVING SKULLS

Early in August 1943, I received 80 inmates [from Auschwitz, whose skulls were to be used for a "subhuman" skull collection]. They were to be killed with the gas [Professor] Hirt had given me. One night I went to the gas chamber in a small car with about 15 women this first time. I told the women they had to go into the chamber to be disinfected. I did not tell them, however, that they were to be gassed.

With the help of a few SS men, I stripped the women completed and shoved them into the gas chamber when they were stark naked. When the door closed they began to scream. I introduced a small amount of salt through a tube . . . and observed through a peephole what happened inside the room. The women breathed for about half a minute before they fell to the floor. After I had turned on the ventilation I opened the door. I found the women lying lifeless on the floor and they were covered with excrements.

I had no feelings in carrying out these things because I had received an order to kill the 80 inmates in the way I already told you. That, by the way, was the way I was trained.

> Josef Kramer
> Describing events of August
> 1943

Testifying at his trial for war crimes.

Revolt at Treblinka

Anyone who came to fetch weapons had to give the password "Death!" to which the proper reply was "Life!" "Death!" "Life!" "Death!" "Life!" Cries of enthusiasm arose as the long-awaited rifles, revolvers and hand grenades were handed out. At the same time the chief murderers of the camp were attacked. Telephone wires were cut and the watchtowers were set on fire with gasoline. . . .

We already had 200 armed men. The others attacked the Germans with axes and spades.

We set fire to the gas chambers, to the "bauhaus," burned the simulated railroad station with all the fake signs . . . "Tickets," "Waiting Room," etc. . . .

Night fell. The battle had already been going on for six hours. The Germans were getting reinforcements and our ranks had become thinner. Our ammunition was running out.

We had been ordered to make for the nearby woods. Most of our fighters fell but there were many German casualties. Very few of us survived.

Shalom Kohn
Treblinka death camp,
Poland
Events of August 2, 1943

From The Death Camp Treblinka: A Documentary, edited by Alexander Donat, 1979.

Treblinka-Bound Trains Run on Time

I was especially pleased to learn from you that already for a fortnight a daily train, taking 5,000 of the Chosen People every time, had gone to Treblinka, so that we are now able to carry out this shifting of population at increased speed. I have contacted the departments concerned myself, so that the smooth carrying out of all these measures seem to be guaranteed.

> Karl Wolff
> Letter to SS superiors
> Treblinka
> August 13, 1943

Cited in The Final Solution *by Gerald Reitlinger.*

A CALL FOR RESISTANCE

Jews, we have nothing to lose.

Death is certain. Who can still believe that he will survive when the murderers kill systematically? The hand of the hangman will reach out to each of us. Neither hiding nor cowardice will save lives.

> Only armed resistance can save our lives and honor. . . .
> Jewish masses
> Out into the streets!
> Those who have no arms get hold of an axe.
> Those who haven't an axe take hold of an iron bar or a
>   cudgel!
> For our murdered children,
> For our parents. . . .
> Strike the murderers!
> In every street, in every yard, in every room, within the
>   ghetto and outside the ghetto.
> Strike the dogs! . . .
> Long live liberty! Long live armed resistance!

> United Partisans Organization
> Proclamation
> Vilna Ghetto, Lithuania
> September 1, 1943

SEPTEMBER 3, 1943

Italy, invaded by Allies, quits war.

DEATH TRAIN

In one of the wagons of the train which left Compiegne for Buchenwald, on the 17th September, 1943, 80 men died out of 130.

> September 17, 1943
> *Nazi Conspiracy and*
> *Aggression*

THE RABBI SOUNDS A WARNING

I have very important news to tell you. Last night I received word that tomorrow the Germans plan to raid Jewish homes throughout Copenhagen to arrest all the Danish Jews for shipment to concentration camps. . . . You must leave the synagogue now and contact all relatives, friends and neighbors you know are Jewish and tell them what I have told you. . . . By nightfall we must all be in hiding.

> Rabbi Marcus Melchior
> Copenhagen synagogue
> September 30, 1943

Cited in Rescue in Denmark *by Harold Flender. Recorded by Rabbi Melchior and used in Flender's documentary film, "An Act of Faith."*

A FIGHT FOR FREEDOM

Notwithstanding our separate religious beliefs, we will fight to preserve for our Jewish brothers and sisters the same freedom we ourselves value more than life.

> Danish Bishops' Proclamation
> October 3, 1943

Cited in Rescue in Denmark *by Harold Flender.*

HIMMLER ADDRESSES SS OFFICERS

This is one of the things that is easily said: "The Jewish people are going to be exterminated," that's what every Party member says, "sure, it's in our program, elimination of the Jews, extermination—it'll be done." And then they all come along, the 80 million worthy Germans, and each one has his one decent Jew. Of course, the others are swine, but this one, he is a first-rate Jew. Of all those who talk like that not one has seen it happen, not one has had to go through with it. Most of you men know what it is like to see 100 corpses, side by side, or 500 or 1,000. To have stood fast through this and—except for cases of human weakness—to have stayed decent that has made us hard. This is an unwritten and never-to-be-written page of glory in our history. . . .

We can say that we have carried out this most difficult of tasks in a spirit of love for our people. And we have suffered no harm to our inner being, our soul, our character.

> Heinrich Himmler
> Speech
> October 4, 1943

CHILDREN AT TEREZIN

Suddenly, a column of bedraggled children appeared, hundreds of them, between the ages of four to twelve years, holding each other's hands. The older ones helped the small ones, their little bodies moving along in the pouring rain. A column of marching ghosts, with wet rags clinging to their emaciated bodies accompanied by a large number of SS men.

Were these the enemies of the Third Reich to be so fiercely guarded? . . .

The children came from Bialistok Ghetto in Poland. . . .

One day, they disappeared in the same way they had

arrived. . . . On Erev Yom Kippur . . . 1,196 children from the Bialistok Ghetto . . . and 53 doctors and nurses from the Terezin Ghetto . . . who accompanied them to the end, said their last *Shema* in the gas chambers of Auschwitz.

Hana Greenfield
Recollecting events of August
24–October 7, 1943
Fragments of Memory, 1992.

The children were apparently to be part of some kind of exchange or ransom deal with the Nazis. The deal fell through.

SOBIBOR REBELLION

October 14 was a clear, sunny day. The night before we distributed the knives that had been gathered and a number of hatchets which the blacksmith made to order for us, small enough to be hidden under a coat. . . . Only the leaders knew when and how we would escape. . . .

The attack on the arsenal did not succeed. A barrage of automatic fire cut us off. The majority of the people made a rush for the central exit. Trampling the guards, firing from the several rifles in their possession, hurling stones at the Fascists they met and blinding them with sand, they pushed through the gate and made for the woods.

Alexander Pechersky
Sobibor concentration
camp
October 14, 1943

Cited in They Fought Back, *edited and translated by Yuri Suhl.*

OCTOBER 16, 1943

A total of 1,127 Jews—more than two-thirds of them women and children—are rounded up in northern Italy. They are shipped to Birkenau concentration camp. Fourteen will survive.

REPORT FROM THE PRECIOUS METALS DEPARTMENT

We all knew that these places [from which gold and jewels were being sent for sale] were the sites of concentration camps. It was in the tenth delivery in November, 1943, that dental gold appeared. The quantity of dental gold became unusually great.

> Manager, Precious Metals
> Department, Reichsbank,
> Frankfurt branch
> Deposition at Nuremberg
> relating to November 1943
> events

STATEMENT ON ATROCITIES

The United Kingdom, the United States and the Soviet Union have received from many quarters evidence of atrocities, massacres and cold-blooded mass executions which are being perpetrated by Hitlerite forces in many of the countries they have overrun and from which they are now being steadily expelled. The brutalities of Hitlerite domination are no new thing and all peoples or territories in their grip have suffered from the worst form of government by terror. What is new is that many of these territories are now being redeemed by the advancing armies of the liberating powers and that in their desperation, the recoiling Hitlerite Huns are redoubling their ruthless cruelties. This is now evidenced with particular clearness by monstrous crimes of the Hitlerites. . . .

Accordingly, the aforesaid three Allied Powers, speaking in the interests of the 33 United Nations, hereby solemnly declare and give full warning of their declaration as follows: At the time of granting of any armistice to any government which may be set up in Germany, those German officers and men and members of the Nazi Party who have been responsible for or have taken a consenting part in the above atrocities, massacres and executions will be sent back to the countries in which their abominable deeds were done in order that they may be judged and punished. . . . Lists will be compiled in all possible detail from all these countries. . . . Thus, Germans who take part in wholesale shooting of Polish officers or in the execution of French, Dutch, Belgian or Norwegian hostages or by Cretan peasants or who have shared in slaughters inflicted on the people of Poland or in territories of the Soviet Union which are now being swept clear of the enemy, will know they will be brought back to the scene of their crimes and judged on the spot by the peoples whom they have outraged. Let those who have hitherto not imbrued their hands with innocent blood beware lest they join the ranks of the guilty, for most assuredly the three Allied Powers will pursue them to the uttermost ends of the earth and will deliver them to their accusers in order that justice may be done.

> President Roosevelt, Prime
> Minister Churchill,
> Premier Stalin
> Statement made public at
> Moscow Conference
> November 1, 1943

Congress: Save Jews from Extinction

[Congress] recommends and urges the creation by the President of a commission of diplomatic, economic, and military experts to formulate and effectuate a plan of immediate action designed to save the surviving Jewish people of Europe from extinction at the hands of Nazi Germany.

> Congressional resolution*
> Washington, D.C.
> Introduced November 9,
> 1943

---

*Resolution did not come to a vote. In January, 1944, President Roosevelt created the War Refugee Board.

HELP FOR ITALIAN JEWS

[The Italian people] sheltered Jews in the villages or smuggled them into the southern part of Italy [occupied by the Allies]. Although the Italian church as a whole had, in the beginning, made little effort to save Jews, individual priests of various orders, in the smaller communities, sheltered Jews in the churches and convents. Later the church as a whole began to help the Jews.

> Masimo Adolfo Vitale
> In *YIVO Bletter*, Vol. 37, 1954
> Events of 1943–45

GERM WARFARE

At the beginning of 1944 in the Ozarichi region of the Belorussian S.S.R., before liberation by the Red Army, the Germans established three concentration camps without shelters, to which they committed tens of thousands of persons from the neighboring territories. They brought many people to these camps from typhus hospitals intentionally, for the purpose of infecting the other persons interned and for spreading the disease in territories from which the Germans were being driven by the Red Army. In these camps there were many murders and crimes.

> Events of 1944
> *Nazi Conspiracy and*
> *Aggression*

JOINING THE ORCHESTRA AT BIRKENAU

The Polish woman opened the door and I entered something closely resembling paradise. There was light and a stove, indeed it was so warm that I could hardly breathe and stood rooted to the spot. Stands, music, a woman on a platform. In front of me pretty girls were sitting, well dressed, with pleated skirts and jerseys, holding musical instruments: violins, mandolins, guitars, flutes, pipes . . . and a grand piano lording it over them all. It couldn't be possible, it wasn't happening. I'd gone mad. No, I was dead, and these were the angels.

> Fania Fenelon
> Birkenau concentration
> camp, Poland
> January 1944

From Playing for Time *by Fania Fenelon with Marcelle Routier, 1977.*

NAKED IN THE STREETS

"What does it mean?" I asked my guide. "Why are they lying there naked?"

"When a Jew dies [in the ghetto]," he answered, "his family removes his clothing and throws his body in the street. If not, they have to pay the Germans to have the body buried. They have instituted a burial tax which practically no one here can afford. Besides, this saves clothing. Here, every rag counts."

> Jan Karski
> *Story of a Secret State*
> 1944

THE BIG LIE: A PREDICTION

They will never believe. They will never believe that the people of Adolf Hitler set up a slaughterhouse and massacred seven million Jews. They won't believe it, and worse, they will pretend to accept the big lie which that loathsome people has spread throughout the war years: "We did not kill the Jews. The Jews died on the way when we were taking them to the concentration camps. This was what was ordained for them. . . . They succumbed because they were weak, a weak and feeble people." They invented these terrible lies for the sake of their allies, to serve as an excuse, an alibi.

> Itzhak Katzenelson
> Diary excerpt
> Vittel camp, France
> 1944

Cited in Encyclopedia of the Holocaust, *edited by Israel Gutman, 1990.*

A Memo to Morgenthau

Report to the Secretary on the Acquiescence of This Government in the Murder of the Jews. . . . [The State Department] is guilty not only of gross procrastination and wilful failure to act, but even of wilful attempts to prevent action from being taken to rescue Jews from Hitler.

> Foreign Funds Control Staff
> Memo to Treasury Secretary
> Henry Morgenthau, Jr.
> January 10, 1944

Surrender Terms for Germany

Ambassador Winant has submitted from the European Advisory Council an advance copy of the points to be made in the terms of surrender of Germany. . . . The proposed terms stipulate "unconditional surrender" and itemize various points incidental to complete occupation and subjugation of Germany, including eradication of laws against the Jews, relinquishment of occupied territory, return to the 1938 boundary of Germany, abolition of the German General Staff, and payment by Germany of the cost of occupation.

> Harry C. Butcher
> Diary excerpt
> London
> January 27, 1944

Cited in My Three Years with Eisenhower, *1946.*

POPE APPEALS TO HORTHY

We are being beseeched in various quarters to do everything in our power in order that, in this noble and chivalrous nation, the sufferings, already so heavy, endured by a large number of unfortunate people, because of their nationality or race, may not be extended and aggravated. As our Father's heart cannot remain insensitive to these pressing supplications by virtue of our ministry of charity which embraces all men, we address Your Highness personally, appealing to your noble sentiments in full confidence that so many unfortunate people may be spared other afflictions and other sorrows.

> Pope Pius XII
> Telegram to Admiral
>   Horthy of Hungary
> March 1944

Admiral Horthy's government was overthrown by the Nazis. A new puppet government took an active role in handing over Hungarian Jews for deportation—and death.

ON THE JEWISH RACE

The Jews are a race which has to be eliminated; whenever we catch one, it is his end.

> Hans Frank
> Diary excerpt
> March 4, 1944

ESCAPEES REPORT ON AUSCHWITZ

It [the gas chamber] holds 2,000 people. . . . When everybody is inside, the heavy doors are closed. Then there is a short pause, presumably to allow the room temperature to rise to a certain level, after which SS men with gas masks climb on the roof, open the traps, and shake down a preparation in powder form out of tin cans, . . . a cyanide mixture of some sort which turns into gas at a certain temperature. After three minutes everyone in the chamber is dead. . . . The chamber is then opened, aired, and the "special squad" [of slave laborers] carts the bodies on flat trucks to the furnace rooms where the burning takes place.

> Rudolf Vrba and Alfred
> Wetzler
> Report to Jewish underground
> in Slovokia
> April 1944

PASSOVER PRAYER AT BERGEN-BELSEN

Our Father in Heaven, behold it is evident and known to You that it is our desire to do Your will and to celebrate the festival of Passover by eating matzah and by observing the prohibition of *hametz* [eating leavened bread]. But our heart is pained that the enslavement prevents us and we are in danger of our lives. Behold, we are prepared and ready to fulfill Your commandment: "And you shall live by them and not die by them." Therefore, our prayer to You is that You may keep us alive and preserve us and redeem us speedily so that we may observe Your statutes and do Your will and serve You with a perfect heart. Amen.

> Prayer to be recited before
>   meals
> Bergen-Belsen
>   concentration camp
> Passover, 1944

First Kiss

I was sitting with Peter on his divan, it wasn't long before his arm went around me. . . . I laid my arm under his. . . .

Now we've sat like this on other occasions, but never so close together. . . . He held me firmly against him, my left shoulder against his chest; already my heart began to beat faster. . . . He soon took my head in his hands and laid it against him once more. Oh, it was so lovely, I couldn't talk much, the joy was too great. He stroked my cheek and arm a bit awkwardly, played with my curls and our heads lay touching . . . I was too happy for words, and I believe he was as well.

We got up. . . . How it came about so suddenly, I don't know, but before we went downstairs he kissed me, through my hair, half on my left cheek, half on my ear; I tore downstairs without looking round, and am simply longing for today.

> Anne Frank
> Diary excerpt
> *The Diary of a Young Girl*
> April 16, 1944

THE JEWS-FOR-TRUCKS DEAL

All I remember is hearing that a million Jews were to be released somewhere in return for ten thousand all-weather trucks and the promise that these trucks would not under any circumstances be used on the Western front. That was the basis of the agreement, I think. . . . I believe Himmler said at the time that he'd be glad to negotiate with Dr. Chaim Weizmann.

> Adolf Eichmann
> Interrogation
> Recalling events of June 1944

Cited in Eichmann Interrogated, *edited by Jochen von Lang.*

On May 17, 1944, two Hungarian Jewish leaders, Joel Brand and Bandi Grosz, leave Budapest. By way of Vienna, they will proceed to Istanbul to meet with Jewish and Allied leaders. They carry Eichmann's offer to swap trucks for the Nazi army—to be used only on the Russian front, Eichmann swears—in exchange for 100,000 Hungarian Jews. Seen as a ploy to split the Western Allies from the Soviet Union, the deal is never seriously considered.

WHITHER HUNGARIAN JEWRY?

A hundred thousand Jews? Whatever in the world would I do with a hundred thousand Jews?

> Lord Moyne
> British High Commissioner
>   for the Middle East
> Attributed
> 1944

Lord Moyne's reaction to a Nazi proposal to swap 100,000 Hungarian Jews for trucks to be used only on the Russian front. Other sources give the figure of a million Jews.

D-DAY PRAYER

Almighty God, our sons, pride of our nation, this day have set upon a mighty endeavor, a struggle to preserve our republic, our religion, and our civilization, and to set free a suffering humanity.

> Franklin D. Roosevelt
> Prayer on the Allied
>   invasion of Europe
> Washington, D.C.
> June 6, 1944

JUNE 9, 1944

Ivar C. Olsen, representative of America's War Refugee Board in Sweden, meets with Raoul Wallenberg in Stockholm. The agenda: saving Hungarian Jews. Wallenberg is to get a diplomatic passport from the government of Sweden, proceed to Budapest with half a million Swedish crowns, and be empowered to issue Swedish passports.

HIMMLER'S VIEW OF THE WAR

The war we are waging is chiefly and essentially a race war. It is first and foremost a war against the Jew, who incited other nation-states, such as England and America, to enter the war against us, and it is, second, a war against Russia. The war against Jewry and the Asiatics is a war between two races.

> Heinrich Himmler
> Speech
> Sonthofen, Germany
> June 21, 1944

AUSCHWITZ BOMBING RULED OUT

The War Department is of the opinion that the suggested air operation [to bomb the rail lines leading to Auschwitz] is impracticable for the reason that it could be executed only by diversion of considerable air support essential to the success of our forces now engaged in decisive operations.

The War Department fully appreciates the humanitarian importance of the suggested operation. However, after due consideration of the problem, it is considered that the most effective relief to victims of enemy persecution is the early defeat of the Axis, an undertaking to which we must devote every resource at our disposal.

> War Department
> Operations Division
> Memorandum
> June 26, 1944

SPEER GETS A WARNING

One day . . . , my friend Karl Hanke, the Gauleiter of Lower Silesia, came to see me. In earlier years he had told me . . . about the Polish and French campaigns, had spoken of . . .

the pain and agonies, and . . . had shown himself a man of sympathy and directness. This time . . . , he seemed confused and spoken falteringly. . . . He advised me never to accept an invitation to inspect a concentration camp in Upper Silesia. Never, under any circumstances. He had seen something there which he was not permitted to describe and moreover could not describe.

I did not query him, I did not query Himmler, I did not query Hitler. . . . I did not investigate—for I did not want to know. . . . Hanke must have been speaking of Auschwitz.

> Albert Speer
> Recollection of
> Summer 1944
> Berlin

From memoirs, Inside the Third Reich, *1970.*

COLD SHOULDER

It is only too true that the Swedish Jews don't want any more Jews in Sweden. They are very comfortably situated here, have no anti-Semitic problems, and are very much afraid that an influx of Jews will not only be a burden to them but will create a Jewish problem in Sweden. Consequently, you will find them very interested in Jewish rescue problems, so long as they do not involve bringing them into Sweden.

> Ivar C. Olsen
> Letter to John W. Pehle,
> Head of the War Refugee
> Board
> Washington, D.C.
> Summer 1944

Cited in Righteous Gentile: The Story of Raoul Wallenberg *by John Bierman, 1981.*

GUESS WHO'S BEING PROMOTED?

In recommending him for promotion . . . , [a superior] spoke
of his "open, honest, firm . . . [and] absolutely dependable
character" and "magnificent" intellectual and physical talents;
of the "discretion, perseverance, and energy with which he has
fulfilled every task . . . and . . . shown himself equal to every situation;" of his "valuable contribution to anthropological
science by making use of the scientific materials available to
him;" of his "absolute ideological firmness" and "faultless
conduct [as] an SS officer;" and of such personal qualities as
"free, unrestrained, persuasive, and lively" discourse that
rendered him "especially dear to his comrades."

> Eduard Wirths
> Recommending promotion
>   for Dr. Josef Mengele
> Auschwitz
> August 1944

From The Nazi Doctors *by Robert Jay Lifton, 1986.*

CONVINCED

Never have I been confronted with such complete evidence
clearly establishing every allegation made by those investigat-
ing German crimes. After inspection of Maidanek, I am now
prepared to believe any story of German atrocities, no matter
how savage, cruel and depraved.

> Bill Lawrence
> *The New York Times*
> August 30, 1944

DECISION FOR A SKULL COLLECTION

As the American army moved toward Strasbourg . . . , [Dr. August] Hirt appealed to Sievers for advice as to what should be done with the cadaver collection of 80-odd bodies that were set aside for the anthropological collection [of skulls]. Hirt was caught on the horns of a dilemma; he would have to choose between protecting the needs of racial science or leaving damning evidence. Specifically, Hirt requested that a decision be made as to whether the collection can be preserved, partly dissolved, or entirely dissolved. . . . The request [was passed] on to Himmler. . . . Hirt was ordered to do away with the bodies completely.

> Frederick H. Kasten
> Citing events of September
> 1944

From his essay, "Unethical Nazi Medicine in Annexed Alsace-Lorraine: The Strange Case of Nazi Anatomist Professor Dr. August Hirt," in Historians and Archivists: Essays in Modern German History and Archival Policy, *edited by George O. Kent.*

OCTOBER 7, 1944

Prisoners at Auschwitz blow up Crematorium
Three. Several Germans are killed.

CHANGES FOR HUNGARIAN JEWS

In connection with the Jewish question which in recent months has given rise to so much excitement among both the Jews and certain circles of their friends, I declare that we shall solve it. This solution—even if ruthless—will be what the Jews deserve by reason of their previous and present conduct. . . . I recognize no letter or safe-conduct of any kind nor any foreign passport which a Jew of Hungarian nationality may have received from whatever source or person.

> Gabor Vajna, Minister of
> Interior
> Decree
> Budapest
> October 18, 1944

CONDITIONS AT BUCHENWALD

Nature's call was answered atop naked dead bodies. . . . Savage struggles to the death took place over the pitiful daily ration. . . . Mess gear was commonly used in place of the latrines, partly from feebleness that made it impossible to leave the barrack, partly from fear of the weather outside or of theft, partly because it was almost impossible to get out of the crowded bunks. Those on top often climbed to the roof, by removing boards and roofing, and fouled the rafters.

> Eugen Kogon
> *The Theory and Practice of
> Hell*
> Citing events of autumn, 1944

Finland Says No

Finland is a decent nation. We would rather perish together with the Jews. We will not surrender them!

> Foreign Minister Witting of
>   Finland
> Addressing an emissary of
>   Heinrich Himmler
> ca. 1944

During World War II, Finland fought the Soviet Union as an ally of Nazi Germany.

Eichmann's Threat

I will kill that Jew-dog Wallenberg!

> Adolf Eichmann
> Budapest
> November 1944

Cited in Righteous Gentile: The Story of Raoul Wallenberg *by John Bierman, 1981.*

EVALUATION OF ATROCITY STORY

Too Semitic.

> U.S. Army officer
> Referring to a story by Sgt.
> Richard Paul for *Yank*. The
> story was based on War
> Refugee Board statistics
> on murdered Jews. It was
> never published.
> November 1944

Cited in Beyond Belief *by Deborah E. Lipstadt.*

WALLENBERG WRITES HOME

The situation here is hectic, fraught with danger, and I am terribly snowed under with work. . . . Night and day we hear the thunder of the approaching Russian guns. Since Szalas came to power [after a Nazi coup] diplomatic activity has been very lively. I myself am almost the sole representative of our embassy.

> Raoul Wallenberg
> Letter to his mother
> Budapest
> December 1944

Cited in Righteous Gentile: The Story of Raoul Wallenberg *by John Bierman,*
> *1981.*

A CONCENTRATION CAMP IN FRANCE

It [the camp at Natzwiller-Struthof in France] might have been a Civilian Conservation Corps camp. From the winding road to the bald hilltop, the sturdy green barrack buildings looked exactly like those that housed forestry trainees in the United States during the early New Deal. . . . One had to force into one's consciousness the fact that this was not a foresters' or lumbermen's camp . . . [but] the charnel-house of the St. Die Valley—the Lublin of Alsace.

> Milton Bracker
> *The New York Times*
> December 5, 1944

BRECKINRIDGE LONG'S TESTIMONY

The most complete exposure of the State Department's failure to do anything about refugees (except keep them out of the country) is perhaps provided in . . . the testimony of Breckinridge Long, the Assistant Secretary of State . . . before the House Foreign Affairs Committee on Nov. 26, 1943. . . .

Long's testimony was partly a smear campaign against American Jews, who he suggested were trying to help Jews at the expense of non-Jews. . . .

Long's other strategy was the use of misleading statistics and actual misstatements. To give the impression of vast numbers of Jewish refugees entering this country, he states: "We have taken into this country since the beginning of Hitler's regime . . . approximately 580,000 refugees." But Long was really talking about *visas issued*, and all visas are not used. Thus the actual number of aliens admitted *from all over the world* . . . in the period was only 477,000; of these 286,000 came from Europe, and of these 166,000 were Jews. . . .

He also defended the disgracefully small number of refugees admitted since Pearl Harbor—i.e., during the time, as we are now learning, . . . that the Jews were being slaughtered on a scale not approached before then. (In . . . 1943, . . .

immigration was cut down so drastically that only 5.9% of the legal quota . . . was filled.) This drop in admissions was explained by Long as due to lack of shipping facilities after the country entered the war. But . . . Spanish and Portuguese ships *alone* which made trips to this country in that period had a capacity of 1,000 to 2,000 a month—as against the average 200 who actually arrived in them each month. The real reason . . . is the restrictive regulations adopted by . . . the State Department, under the pretext of keeping out Gestapo spies, notably the almost incredible provision that *no one with relatives in Axis-occupied Europe was eligible for admission.*

> Dwight Macdonald
> *Politics*
> January 1945

From Memoirs of a Revolutionist, *1957.*

As Liberation Nears, a Death March to the Sea

Darkness all around—we did not know where we were going. We were divided into groups. Then we were led through bushes and undergrowth. . . . We were promised that we would not be shot—we should just walk along quietly, we were being brought by sea to Estonia to work there. . . . No need to be afraid.

Then a Jewish prisoner came and said under his breath: "You do not know what they are doing with us. We are being separated off into groups and thrown into ice holes."

Then a German ran up to me, took me by the collar and threw me into the sea. Our whole group was already inside the water. Several women were shot. . . . I lay on a block of frozen ice and the body of a woman who had been shot was thrown on top of me. It turned out that the people were being thrown into the sea, alive. At shallow spots along the shore there was a cover of ice . . . but people screamed, begging to be shot.

Eyewitness account
January 31, 1945

Cited in "Evacuation of the Stutthof Concentration Camp" by Olga Picknolz-Barnitsch, Yad Vashem Bulletin, December 1965.

DEATH MARCH

In April, 1945, of 12,000 internees evacuated from Buchenwald, 4,000 only were still alive when the marching column arrived near Regensburg.

*Nazi Conspiracy and
Aggression*
April 1945

ENDING A MEDICAL EXPERIMENT

Like pictures hung up on a wall on hooks.

Prisoner
Bullenhausendamm camp
April 1945

Describing how children, who had been subjected to tuberculosis experiments, looked like after they were hanged by the Nazis. They were murdered to dispose of any evidence.

Cited in The Theory and Practice of Hell *by Eugen Kogon.*

BRITISH LIBERATE BERGEN-BELSEN

Toward us came what seemed to me to be the remnants of a Holocaust—a tottering mass of blackened skin and bones, held together somehow with filthy rags. "My God, the dead are walking!"

> Chaplain Leslie Hardman
> Bergen-Belsen
> April 15, 1945

Cited in The Survivors *by Leslie Hardman.*

EISENHOWER ISSUES AN ORDER

We are told that the American soldier does not know what he is fighting for. Now, at least, he will know what he is fighting *against*.

> General Dwight Eisenhower
> Statement on ordering
>   American troops to tour a
>   liberated concentration
>   camp
> Ohrdruf, Germany
> April 12, 1945

AFTER VIEWING BUCHENWALD

We are constantly finding German camps in which they have placed political prisoners where unspeakable conditions exist.

From my own personal observation, I can state unequivocally that all written statements up to now do not paint the full horrors.

>Dwight Eisenhower
>Telegram to Washington
>   and London
>Third Army Headquarters,
>   Germany
>April 1945

G.I. AT NORDHAUSEN

[The concentration camp inmates] were so thin they didn't have anything—didn't have any buttocks to lie on; there wasn't any flesh on their arms to rest their skulls on. . . . One man . . . had died on his knees with his arms and head in a praying position.

>William B. Lovelady
>Nordhausen, Germany
>Reporting events of April
>   1945

Cited in the Fred R. Crawford Witness to the Holocaust Project.

MURROW AT BUCHENWALD

When I entered [the concentration camp], men crowded around, tried to lift me to their shoulders. They were too weak. . . . As I walked down to the end of the barracks, there was applause from the men too weak to get out of bed. It sounded like the handclapping of babies, they were so weak.

Edward R. Murrow
Radio broadcast
Buchenwald
April 1945

Cited in Prime Time: The Life of Edward R. Murrow, *1969.*

RAVENSBRUCK TO COPENHAGEN

The commandant of the camp told us not to breathe a word about what was going on in Ravensbruck. And we said no, no, we wouldn't say anything. . . .

We traveled through war-torn Germany without stopping during the day. There were bombs falling everywhere. It took us three days to get to Denmark. We arrived on April 28 [1945], late at night. Denmark was still occupied by the Germans but they didn't stop us anywhere. We were put on Pullman trains and when we came out in Copenhagen it seemed that the whole population of the city was there to greet us. We were the first inmates of concentration camps to arrive. There were about seventeen hundred of us. I remember seeing people with children on their shoulders, and they were throwing flowers at us. There were photographers everywhere taking our pictures.

Sally Grubman
Voices from the Holocaust
Edited by Sylvia Rothchild
Events of April 1945

INCIDENT AT A RAILROAD SIDING

Several [U.S. Army] units converged on the railroad siding that serviced the [Dachau concentration] camp there to find about forty open freight cars filled with more than 2,000 corpses, the tangle of bodies laced with remnants of striped uniforms and the stench of excrement and death.

> Robert H. Abzug
> *Inside the Vicious Heart*
> Citing events of April 29,
>   1945

Mauthausen Liberated

The day was sunny, with the scent of spring in the air. Gone was the sweetish smell of burned flesh that had always hovered over the yard. The night before, the last SS men had run away. The machinery of death had come to a stop. In my room a few dead people were lying on their bunks.

> Simon Wiesenthal
> *Hunter and the Hunted* by
>   Gerd Korman
> Citing events of May 8, 1945

MAY 8, 1945

Germany surrenders to the Allies. The war in Europe is over.

EICHMANN'S COUNT

Approximately 4 million Jews had been killed in the various concentration camps, while an additional 2 million met death in other ways, the major part of which were shot by operational squads of the Security Police during the campaign against Russia.

According to my knowledge, [Adolf] Eichmann was at that time the leader of the Jewish Section of the Gestapo, and in addition to that he had been ordered by Himmler to get a hold of the Jews in all the European countries to transport them to Germany. Eichmann was then very much impressed with the fact that Rumania had withdrawn from the war in those days. Moreover, he had come to me to get information about the military situation which I received daily from the Hungarian Ministry of War and from the Commander of the Waffen-SS in Hungary. He [Eichmann] expressed his conviction that Germany had now lost the war and that he personally had no other chance. He knew that he would be considered one of the main war criminals by the United Nations, since he had millions of Jewish lives on his conscience. I asked him how many that was, to which he answered that although the number was a great Reich secret, he would tell me since I, as a historian, would be interested, and that he would probably not return anyhow from his command in Rumania. He had, shortly before that, made a report to Himmler, as the latter wanted to know the exact number of Jews who had been killed.

Dr. Wilhelm Hoettl
Deputy Group Leader of
the Foreign Section of
the Security Section

Affidavit to the International Military Tribunal at Nuremberg, 1945.

AT WAR'S END, HITLER'S LEGACY

Auschwitz, Belzec, Bergen-Belsen, Birkenau, Buchenwald, Chelmo, Dachau, Flossenburg, Gross-Rosen, Majdanek, Mauthausen, Natzweiler, Neuengamme, Nordhausen, Ravensbruck, Sachsenhausen, Sobibor, Struthof, Terezin, Treblinka.

AFTERMATH

THE DEATH CAMPS

Methods used for the work of extermination in concentration camps were: bad treatment, pseudo-scientific experiments (sterilization of women at Auschwitz and at Ravensbruck, study of the evolution of cancer of the womb at Auschwitz, of typhus at Buchenwald, anatomical research at Natzweiller, heart injections at Buchenwald, bone grafting and muscular excisions at Ravensbruck, etc.), gas chambers, gas wagons and crematory ovens.

> International Military
> Tribunal
> Indictment
> Nuremberg
> October 1945

ON GERMAN GUILT

A thousand years will pass and the guilt of Germany will not be erased.

> Hans Frank
> Nuremberg War Crimes Trial
> 1945

NUREMBERG INDICTMENT

The defendants, with diverse other persons, are guilty of a common plan of conspiracy for accomplishment of crimes against peace—against humanity—war crimes not only against armed forces of their enemies but also against nonbelligerent civilian populations.

> International War Crimes
> Tribunal
> First count of indictment
> Nuremberg, Germany
> November 20, 1945

Of the 21 top Nazi leaders who stood trial, 18 were convicted. Eleven of these were sentenced to be hanged.

FRANK AT NUREMBERG

There must be some basic evil in me. In all men. Mass hypnosis. "Hitler cultivated this evil in man. When I saw him in that movie in court, I was swept along again for a moment, in spite of myself. Funny, one sits in court feeling guilt and shame. Then Hitler appears on the screen and you want to stretch out your hand to him. . . . It's not with horns on his head or a forked tail that the devil comes to us, you know. He comes with a captivating smile, spouting idealistic sentiments, winning one's loyalty. We cannot say that Adolf Hitler violated the German people. He seduced us.

> Hans Frank
> Interview with Nuremberg
> Psychologist Gustav
> Gilbert
> Late 1945

Cited in Nuremberg: Infamy on Trial *by Joseph E. Persico, 1994.*

FILM SHOWN AT NUREMBERG

At this point [in the trial] a strip of motion picture footage taken, presumably, by a member of the SS, and captured by the United States military forces in an SS barracks near Augsburg, Germany, was shown to the tribunal. The film depicts what is believed to be the extermination of a ghetto by Gestapo agents, assisted by military units.

The following scenes are representative:

SCENE 2:   A naked girl running across the courtyard.

SCENE 3:   An older woman being pushed past the camera, and a man in SS uniform standing at the right of the scene.

SCENE 5:   A man with a skull cap and a woman are manhandled.

SCENE 14:   A half-naked woman runs through the crowd.

SCENE 15:   Another half-naked woman runs out of the house.

SCENE 16:   Two men drag an old man out.

SCENE 18:   A man in German military uniform, with his back to the camera, watches.

SCENE 24:   A general shot of the street, showing fallen bodies and naked women running.

SCENE 32:   A shot of the street, showing five fallen bodies.

SCENE 37:   A man with a bleeding head is hit again.

SCENE 44:   A soldier with a rifle, in German military uniform, walks past a woman clinging to a torn blouse.

SCENE 45:   A woman is dragged by her hair across the street.

> Nuremberg trial exhibit
> *Nazi Conspiracy and*
> *Aggression*

NUREMBERG IQ's

Results of the Wechsler-Bellevue Adult Intelligence Test taken by some of the defendants at Nuremberg:

Highest: Schacht, with 143. Others included Seyss-Inquart, 140; Goering, 138; Frank, 130; and Speer, 128. Lowest of all was Streicher, with 106.

Nuremberg
Late 1945

Statistics from Nuremberg: Infamy on Trial *by Joseph E. Persico, 1994.*

The Nuremberg Verdicts

Death: Hermann Goering, Joachim von Ribbentrop, Wilhelm Keitel, Ernst Kaltenbrunner, Alfred Rosenberg, Hans Frank, Wilhelm Frick, Julius Streicher, Fritz Sauckel, Alfred Jodl, Artur Seyss-Inquart, Martin Bormann.
      Life imprisonment: Rudolf Hess, Walther Funk, Erich Raeder.
      Twenty years imprisonment: Baldur von Schirach, Albert Speer.
      Fifteen years imprisonment: Constantin von Neurath.
      Ten years imprisonment: Karl Doenitz.
      Acquitted: Halmar Schacht, Franz von Papen, Hans Fritsche.

International Military
Tribunal
Nuremberg
October 1, 1946

Bormann, tried in absentia, could not be found after the war. He either escaped to South America or died during the siege of Berlin.

Niemoeller Commentary

First they came for the communists, but I was not a communist—so I said nothing.

Then they came for the social democrats, but I was not a social democrat—so I did nothing.

Then came the trade unionists, but I was not a trade unionist.

And then they came for the Jews, I was not a Jew—so I did little.

Then when they came for me there was no one left who could stand up for me.

Rev. Martin Niemoeller
Postwar speaking tour

*Cited in "Martin Niemoeller, Activist as Bystander: The Oft-Quoted Reflection,"
an essay by Ruth Zerner in* Jewish-Christian Encounters Over the Centuries,
*edited by Marvin Perry and Frederick M. Schweitzer. There are a number of
versions of this quotation. This is Ruth Zerner's translation of a version
furnished by Niemoeller's widow.*

POSTWAR POLAND

On July 4 [1946] a crowd of Poles, aroused by rumours of Jews abducting Christian children for ritual purposes, attacked the building of the Jewish Committee in Kielce. Almost all the Jews who were inside the building, including the chairman of the Committee, Dr. Seweryn Kahane, were shot, stoned to death, or killed with axes and blunt instruments. Elsewhere in Kielce, Jews were murdered in their homes, or dragged into the streets and killed by the mob. Forty-two Jews were killed in Kielce that day.

Events of July 4, 1946
The Holocaust by Martin
Gilbert

PERKINS ON ROOSEVELT

The aggressions against the Jewish people in Germany filled him [Roosevelt] with horror. They seemed to him almost unbelievable. He was inclined to think they were the work of gangsters, like the fanatical organizations in the United States which took, in times past, a violent attitude toward one minority group or another.

But continued reports from our ambassadors and from occasional refugees convinced him that this was an approved program of the German government itself. He saw that it might grow rather than decline. He saw that it was Evil rampant.

> Frances Perkins
> *The Roosevelt I Knew*
> 1946

CONDEMNED TO HANG, GOERING TAKES POISON

If it had been a firing squad [to carry out his execution] instead of hanging, my father would probably have gone to his. That would have been like a soldier. But hanging was like a criminal. It took much strength to kill himself. I will always be grateful to the man who did this for us. [Presumably, smuggled the poison in to Goering.]

> Edda Goering
> Commenting on her father's
>   suicide which had taken
>   place on October 15,
>   1946

From Hitler's Children: Sons and Daughters of Leaders of the Third Reich Talk About Their Fathers and Themselves *by Gerald L. Posner.*

NOVEMBER 1947

United Nations votes to partition Palestine
into Jewish and Arab states. Jews accept,
Arabs reject, the plan.

JUSTIFICATION FOR GENOCIDE

Out of respect for human life, I would remove a purulent appendix from a diseased body. The Jew is the purulent appendix in the body of Europe.

Dr. Fritz Klein
SS doctor at Auschwitz

Cited in Prisoners of Fear, *by Dr. Ella Lingens-Reiner, 1948.*

DECEMBER 9, 1948

United Nations approves the International
Convention on the Prevention and
Punishment of Genocide.

HECHT COMMENTARY

The silence [during the Holocaust] shamed me. It contained for me an anti-Semitism more sinister than the massacre. I felt the most deeply shamed by the silence of the American Jews. Around me the most potent and articulate Jews in the world kept their mouths fearfully closed.

The unassimilated Jews—the Yiddish Jews—were speaking their horror in the Jewish newspapers. In the synagogues the Jews were weeping and praying. In thousands of homes where Yiddish was spoken the German murderers and their deeds were cursed. But these were the locked-away Jews who had only the useless ear of other Jews and, possibly, of God.

The Americanized Jews who ran newspapers and movie studios, who wrote plays and novels, who were high in government and powerful in the financial, industrial and even social life of the nation were silent.

Ben Hecht
A Child of the Century
1954

DECEMBER 25, 1959

On Christmas day, a swastika is painted on a synagogue in Cologne, Germany. Similar desecrations follow all over the world.

How Students View Adolf

Surveys made just recently in German schools reveal that most students remember Hitler as the man who built the Autobahns and licked the unemployment problem.

> *Our Age*
> Volume 1, No. 7
> January 31, 1960

A German History Textbook

There were 15 pages devoted to the Third Reich, and they were filled with incredible stories about a mass movement called National Socialism which started out splendidly and ended in a catastrophe for the whole world.

And then there was an extra chapter, about three-quarters of a page long. It was titled "The Extermination of the Jews," and I had read it in my room at home many times. I always locked the door because I didn't want anybody to know what I was reading. Six million Jews were killed. . . . What monsters must have existed then.

> Sabine Reichel
> Recalling events of 1960

From What Did You Do in the War, Daddy?: Growing Up German.

The Fuehrer's Order

The final solution itself—I mean the special mission given to Heydrich—to put it bluntly, the extermination of the Jews, was

not provided for by Reich law. It was a Fuehrer's Order. . . .
And Himmler and Heydrich and Pohl, the head of Administration and Supply—each had his own part in the implementation of this Fuehrer's Order. According to the then prevailing
interpretation, which no one questioned, the Fuehrer's orders
had the force of law. Not only in this case. In every case.

> Adolf Eichmann
> Interrogation
> Jerusalem
> 1960

Cited in Eichmann Interrogated, *edited by Jochen von Lang.*

Hilberg Commentary

The missionaries of Christianity had said in effect: You have no
right to live among us as Jews. The secular rulers who followed
had proclaimed: You have no right to live among us. The
German Nazis at last decreed: You have no right to live.

> Raul Hilberg
> *The Destruction of the*
> *European Jews*
> 1961

Eichmann Has Dreams

I asked the Gruppenfuehrer: "Please do not send me there [to
the sites of the mass killings], send someone else, someone

stronger than I am. You see, I was never sent to the front, I was never a soldier; there are other men who can look upon such actions. I cannot. At night I cannot sleep, I dream. I cannot do it, Gruppenfuehrer."

Adolf Eichmann
Testimony at his trial in
Jerusalem
April 19, 1961

A CALL FOR RECOGNITION

There is something left unsaid [at the Eichmann trial] which only Israel and the Jewish people can and must say and do. History has a claim upon us to balance the moral asymmetry which has distorted the image of man. . . .

We must testify to the acts of sacrifice of thousands of non-Jews who risked their lives to defend and protect the hunted and pursued of our people.

Shall evil be recorded and made known and goodness be buried, silent in neglect?

Rabbi Harold M. Schulweiss
ca. 1962

Cited in Our Age *(April 21, 1963), Volume 4, No. 13.*

THE SUBJECT IS HATRED

I cry out with all my heart against forgiveness, against forgetting, against silence. Every Jew, somewhere in his being, should set apart a zone of hate—healthy, virile hate—for the German. To do otherwise would be a betrayal of the dead.

Elie Wiesel
In the article "An
    Appointment with Hate,"
Commentary
December 1962

Watching a Documentary on the Nazis

It was beyond me. I stared in disbelief at the mock opera unfolding in front of me on the television screen, thinking, "This wasn't for real. It had to be a joke." . . . How come the entire German nation didn't die laughing? . . .

The storm troopers with their silly caps strapped under their square chins and a nasty little smirk on their lips were nothing compared to the ridiculous nincompoop wrapped in brown poplin. . . . This character with a thin, dyspeptic mouth, a greasy fringe over his forehead, and a theater prop for a mustache was obviously a creepy lunatic—the very picture of a coarse, pathetic, and pompous megalomaniac.

Sabine Reichel
Recalling events of the early
    1960s

From What Did You Do in the War, Daddy?: Growing Up German.

Flender Commentary

The Danish people were not alone in acting heroically and effectively in saving their Jewish population. In every country under Nazi control, including Germany, there were individual

acts of courage and humanity that constitute a resounding *Yes!*
to the question *Am I my brother's keeper?* . . . It was only in
Denmark that almost everyone, from King to fisherman, took
an active role in rescuing the Jews. It was only in Denmark that
after World War II over 98.5 percent of the Jews were still alive.

> Harold Flender
> *Rescue in Denmark*
> 1963

ARENDT ON BEN-GURION'S LESSONS

In Ben-Gurion's own words [on the reasons for the Eichmann
trial], "We want the nations of the world to know . . . and
they should be ashamed." The Jews in the Diaspora were to
remember how Judaism, "four thousand years old, with its
spiritual creations and its ethical strivings" had always faced
"a hostile world," how the Jews had degenerated until they
went to their death like sheep, and how only the establishment
of a Jewish state had enabled Jews to hit back, as Israelis had
done. . . . And if the Jews outside Israel had to be shown
the difference between Israeli heroism and Jewish submissive
meekness, there was a lesson for those inside Israel too: "the
generation of Israelis who have grown up since the holocaust"
were in danger of losing their ties with the Jewish people and,
by implication, with their own history.

> Hannah Arendt
> *Eichmann in Jerusalem*
> 1963

EICHMANN: "TERRIFYINGLY NORMAL"

Mr. Hausner [the Israeli prosecutor of Adolf Eichmann] wanted
to try the most abnormal monster the world had ever seen. . . .
It would have been very comforting indeed to believe that

Eichmann was a monster. . . . Surely, one can hardly call upon the whole world and gather correspondents from the four corners of the earth in order to display Bluebeard in the dock. The trouble with Eichmann was precisely that so many were like him, and that the many were neither perverted nor sadistic, that they were, and still are, terribly and terrifyingly normal.

> Hannah Arendt
> *Eichmann in Jerusalem*
> 1963

COULD A HOLOCAUST HAPPEN IN AMERICA?

Germany in modern times was an extremely nationalistic country. The Jews were the only exception as a national minority ethnic group. America is a nation of nations—a conglomeration of all sorts of racial and religious groups, none in the majority. Even the Anglo-Saxons are a minority.

The second major difference is the absence from the American scene of a well-organized political anti-Semitism. In Germany, anti-Semitism was a paramount feature from the Middle Ages. . . . No one in the United States Congress . . . has been elected on the basis of an anti-Semitic program. The German Parliament always had . . . a certain number elected on anti-Semitic platforms.

Unlike England and France, Germany never expelled Jews totally; anti-Semitism never had an intermission. . . . There is no tradition of anti-Semitism in America. My prediction would be that it probably will not happen, but no one can say it can't happen—that is not a historic category.

> Dr. Salo Baron
> Interview in *Our Age,* Volume
> 7, No. 2
> October 31, 1965

The Vatican Denounces Anti-Semitism

True, authorities of the Jews and those who followed their lead pressed for the death of Christ, still, what happened in His passion cannot be blamed upon all the Jews then living, without distinction, nor upon the Jews of today. Although the Church is the new people of God, the Jews should not be presented as repudiated or cursed by God, as if such views followed from the holy Scriptures. All should take pains, then, lest in catechetical instruction and in the preaching of God's Word they teach anything out of harmony with the truth of the gospel and the Christ.

The Church repudiates all persecutions against any man. Moreover, mindful of her common patrimony with the Jews, and motivated by the gospel's spiritual love and by no political considerations, she deplores the hatred, persecutions, and displays of anti-Semitism directed against the Jews at any time and from any source.

> Declaration on the
> Relationship of the
> Church to Non-Christian
> Religions
> Vatican II
> Rome
> October 1965

Davidson Commentary

[The Nuremberg] trials were intended not only to bring the guilty to justice but to make clear to Germans and their conquerors as well how a great *Kulturvolk* whose science, music, scholarship, philosophy, and literature had been in the forefront of mankind's creative achievements had come to its moral and political collapse.

> Eugene Davidson
> *The Trial of the Germans*
> 1966

THE SS: WARNING AND CHALLENGE

In one of these prison-camp discussions [by former members of the SS who were being detained after the war], the former SS-Untersturmfuehrer Erich Kernmayr shouted . . . "We were intoxicated by a vision of world power. It gripped the people like a great frenzy."

So the bloody history of the SS is but another page in that of the old German nation-state, the acts and deeds of the SS are but an illustration of the hypertrophy of nationalism and state omnipotence.

Have the Germans, and have the ex-SS-men, learnt their lesson?

The historian would not make so bold as to give an answer. But the questions remain and will continue to nag at us. For one thing is certain—the history of the SS will continue to stalk the Germans, a record of terrifying lust for power. So long as Germany has a future, that history will stand as a warning and a challenge.

Heinz Hohne
The Order of the Death's Head
Translated from the German by Richard Barry
1966

CONSIDERING REPARATIONS

How can I take money for my sister the "Field Whore" from you—and not be a pimp?

Ka-tzetnik 135633
"Wiedergutmachung" (Reparations)
in *Star Eternal*, 1971

The initials K. Z. stood for the German words "Konzentration Zenter" (concentration camp). The German pronunciation of the letters K. Z. was Ka-Tzet, and an inmate was identified by a Ka-tzetnik number, which was tattooed on the arm.

FEST COMMENTARY

If Hitler had succumbed to an assassination or an accident at the end of 1938, few would hesitate to call him one of the greatest of German statesmen, the consummator of Germany's history. The aggressive speeches and *Mein Kampf,* the anti-Semitism and the design for world dominion, would presumably have fallen into oblivion, dismissed as the man's youthful fantasies, and only occasionally would critics remind an irritated nation of them. Six and one-half years separated Hitler from such renown. Granted, only premature death could have given him that, for by nature he was headed toward destruction and did not make an exception of himself. Can we call him great?

> Joachim C. Fest
> *Hitler*
> 1973

"A MODERN FAIRY TALE"

Once upon a time there were gas chambers and crematoria, and no one lived happily ever after.

> Lawrence L. Langer
> *The Holocaust and the*
>   *Literary Imagination*
> 1975

DAWIDOWICZ COMMENTARY

The idea of a mass annihilation of the Jews had already been adumbrated by apocalyptic-minded anti-Semites during the 19th century. Yet even the most fanatic and uncompromising anti-Semites, when confronted with political actualities and social realities, invariably settled for an aggregation of exclusionary measures. Hitler did not. He succeeded in transforming the apocalyptic idea into concrete political action. The mass murder of the Jews was the consummation of his fundamental beliefs and ideological conviction. . . . For Hitler's ideas about the Jews were the starting place for the elaboration of a monstrous racial ideology that would justify mass murder whose like history had not seen before.

Lucy S. Dawidowicz
The War Against the Jews
1975

HOLOCAUST? WHAT HOLOCAUST?

Obvious lies . . . ludicrous . . . breathtakingly absurd . . . absolutely insane . . . fishy . . . obviously spurious . . . nonsense.

Arthur R. Butz
The Hoax of the 20th Century
1976

WELLS COMMENTARY

As a witness, I am compelled to tell the story of the Holocaust. Yet, I am questioning how it can be done so as not to create the situation where the horrible becomes the familiar; where love of macabre cruelty becomes the most prized pleasures to a certain group of people while others are led to desperation with no hope for humanity. All of these may lead to a self-fulfilling prophecy for another Holocaust on a global scale even while smaller tragedies keep happening.

With the Holocaust, I am grieved to say, we have already established a new criterion for any barbarism. How often does one hear about a mass killing and someone will say, "But they did not use gas chambers." Did we accept this as a definition and criterion for a Holocaust when we should be concerned about any atrocity perpetrated on fellow human beings?

> Leon W. Wells
> "A Survivor's Testimony"
> An essay in *Human Responses*
> *to the Holocaust*
> Edited by Michael D. Ryan

Paper presented at 1979 conference.

FEIG COMMENTARY

The Germans were cruel, but others have been cruel. They were barbaric, but others have been also. The greatest crime of the Germans was their coldblooded systemic scheme to destroy the humanity of their victims. The calculated dehumanization of human beings is so very difficult to understand, to forget, and possibly to forgive. It was an unnatural kind of evil—a satanic rationality in the midst of the madness, a "scarcely governed ache for savagery."

> Konnilyn G. Feig
> *Hitler's Death Camps*
> 1979

GOLD RUSH AT AUSCHWITZ

After the war, prospectors descended on the area [of Auschwitz] with their shovels and pans, and were joined by a new professional class of grave robbers who specialized in excavating the remains of the dead and their hidden treasures. They dug up the camp area again and again, looking for gold and treasure and finding it. Early visitors saw clusters of men hunched over a creek, sifting, panning, washing the day's haul of bones and ashes—a Polish Klondike.

> Konnilyn G. Feig
> *Hitler's Death Camps*
> 1979

WAITE COMMENTARY

At the outset I want to emphasize the central place of anti-Semitism both in Adolf Hitler's personal life and in his public policy. Hatred of the Jewish people and determination to destroy them was not an aberration of his government. It was essential to it. Anti-Semitism and the leadership principle were the two distinguishing features of the German variety of fascism. His government was conceived in oppression and dedicated to the proposition that all men are created unequal, and that the Jews were to be defamed, persecuted, and destroyed. That was the theory. It was also the practice. Never in human history has practice been more consistent with theory.

> Robert G. L. Waite
> "The Perpetrator: Hitler and
> the Holocaust"
> Essay in *Human Responses to
> the Holocaust*, edited by
> Michael D. Ryan

Paper presented at 1979 conference.

Loving the Fuehrer

What is funneled into you in your youth, maybe "We love our
Fuehrer . . ." So! We did love our Fuehrer, really! It was true.
And when that's inside you as a young person, it doesn't leave
so quickly. . . . Nonsense, *gel?* When I see him today, it's
always a wonder it was possible not to see through this human
being.

> Ellen Frey
> Interview
> Munich suburb
> 1980s

Quoted in Frauen: German Women Recall the Third Reich *by Alison Owings.*

Auschwitz as Metaphor

It was to be anticipated that Auschwitz would become a
metaphor and a paradigm for evil. How could it be otherwise?
But what was unexpected was the occasional attempt to turn
Auschwitz into a metaphor for the "ecumenical nature" of the
evil that was committed there or to render the murder of the
Jews as mere atrocity, sheer blood lust. What was unexpected
was the failure to understand—or to acknowledge—that the
evil was not ecumenical, that the killing was not blood lust for
its own sake, but that the evil and killing were specifically
directed against particular victims. To make Auschwitz serve
as the paradigm for universal evil is in effect to deny the
historical reality that the German dictatorship had a specific
intent in murdering the Jews.

> Lucy S. Dawidowicz
> *The Holocaust and the*
> *Historians*
> 1981

Cohn Commentary

The *Protocols* and the myth of the Jewish world-conspiracy were exploited in Nazi propaganda at every stage, from the first emergence of the party in the early 1920s to the collapse of the Third Reich in 1945. They were exploited first to help the party to power—then to justify a regime of terror—then to justify war—then to justify genocide—and finally to postpone surrender to the Allies.

Norman Cohn
Warrant for Genocide
1981

Rothchild Commentary

Whether silent or outspoken, survivors were torn between remembering and forgetting, between shielding their children from their unhappy history and warning them that the world was a dangerous place. They urged each other to "forget the gruesome things . . . and look forward and see the good," but the speed with which the Holocaust was eased into ancient history frightened them.

Sylvia Rothchild
Voices from the Holocaust
1981

Israeli Poll on the Germans

Are all Germans today guilty of the Holocaust?
    No   41 percent
    Yes   9 percent
    Undecided 50 percent

Public Opinion Research
Institute of Israel
Survey
Sampling of Israeli Jews
March 1982

Cited in Eternal Guilt? *by Michael Wolffsohn.*

Bergmann Commentary

I think the Nazi Holocaust must be remembered and compre-
hended, for not to do so would be a huge and dangerous
denial. But a group that only dedicates itself to the past is
traumatized and never allows complete mourning to take
place. To be traumatized and in mourning inevitably affects a
group's ability to assess current threats and deal with them
effectively and realistically. Therefore, we have to steer a careful line between not forgetting and excessive remembering.

Too much stress on remembrance is an oppressive way to
live. It is often overlooked that the process of mourning should
ultimately lead to some measure of resolution and resignation
without despair.

Martin S. Bergmann
Roundtable discussion on
"Psychoanalysis and the
Holocaust"
May 2, 1982

From Psychoanalytic Reflections on the Holocaust, *edited by Steven A. Luel
and Paul Marcus.*

MARRUS AND PAXTON COMMENTARY

In the summer and autumn of 1942, when the French police and administration lent their hands to the task, some 42,500 Jews were deported from France to their deaths—perhaps one-third of them at Vichy's initiative from the Unoccupied Zone. When Vichy began to drag its feet in 1943, the number declined to 22,000 sent east in the year 1943. After the last use of French police in January 1944, and despite feverish last-minute German efforts, the number deported up to August 1944 was 12,500. One can only speculate how many fewer would have perished if the Nazis had been obliged to identify, arrest, and transport without any French assistance every Jew in France which they wanted to slaughter.

> Michael R. Marrus and
> Robert O. Paxton
> *Vichy France and the Jews*
> 1983

CRITICIZING THE DRAMA OF ANNE'S DIARY

The authors of the dramatic version of Anne Frank's *Diary* lacked artistic will—or courage—to leave their audiences over-whelmed by the feeling that Anne's bright spirit was extin-guished, that Anne, together with millions of others, was killed simply because she was Jewish, and for no other reason. That Anne herself, had she survived, would have been equal to this challenge is suggested by her brief description of a roundup of Amsterdam Jews witnessed from her attic window. . . .

But the audience in the theater is sheltered from this somber vision, lest it disrupt the mood of carefully orches-trated faith in human nature that swells into a crescendo just before the play's climax, when the Gestapo and Green Police arrive to arrest the inhabitants of the annex.

> Lawrence L. Langer
> Essay "The Americanization
>   of the Holocaust on Stage
>   and Screen"
> *From Hester Street to*
>   *Hollywood,* edited by
>   Susan Blacher Cohen,
>   1983

Hanson Commentary

The Holocaust happened because Western Europe's most industrially advanced nation became powerful enough to act as a delegate of European anti-Semitism and racist nationalism. Its monstrosities were systematized by the German forebrain and rationalized—even beautified—by a conservative, antimodernist culture that Germany had evolved to mask its own social and psychological fall into modernity. Self-hatred, inferiority externalized in a war on "enemies" who had to be big enough to inflate the devalued ego of the aggressive followers of Nazism. At its heart, Nazi culture, with its knights and demigods, was an idealized act of destruction.

> John H. Hanson
> "Nazi Culture: The Social
>   Uses of Fantasy as
>   Repression"
> *Psychoanalytic Reflections*
>   *on the Holocaust*
> edited by Steven A. Luel
>   and Paul Marcus
> 1984

SOUNDS OF SILENCE

Despite his proclaimed Zionism, Winston Churchill had his mind on other things during the war, and he allowed the Jewish question to be dealt with by subordinates, who wished to prevent the immigration of more Jewish refugees into Palestine. For his part, Roosevelt chose not to make persecution of Jews a central issue because he feared it would erode support for the war effort.

> Arthur J. Goldberg and
> Arthur Hertzberg
> Article
> *Los Angeles Times*
> March 1984

WYMAN COMMENTARY

The Holocaust was certainly a Jewish tragedy, but it was not *only* a Jewish tragedy. It was also a Christian tragedy, a tragedy for Western civilization, and a tragedy for all humankind. The killing was done by people to other people, while still other people stood by. The perpetrators, where they were not actually Christians, arose from a Christian culture. The bystanders most capable of helping were Christians. The point should have been obvious. Yet comparatively few American non-Jews recognized that the plight of the European Jews was their plight too. Most were either unaware, did not care, or saw the European Jewish catastrophe as a Jewish problem, one for Jews to deal with. That explains, in part, why the United States did so little to help.

Would the reaction be different today? Would Americans be more sensitive, less self-centered, more willing to make sacrifices, less afraid of differences now than they were then?

> David S. Wyman
> *The Abandonment of the Jews*
> 1984

ROOSEVELT AND THE JEWS

Roosevelt's grasp of Jewish issues tended to be superficial. To note but one example, during the Casablanca Conference he spoke for keeping the number of Jewish professionals in North America proportional to the Jewish population there. This, he stated, would avoid the "understandable complaints which the Germans bore towards the Jews in Germany, namely, that while they represented a small part of the population, over fifty percent of the lawyers, doctors, school teachers, college professors, etc., in Germany were Jews." . . . In reality, Jews had composed 1 to 2 percent of Germany's population. They had occupied 2.3 percent of professional positions. In the extreme cases, lawyers and medical doctors, Jews made up 16.3 and 10.9 percent respectively. They held 2.6 percent of the professorships and 0.5 percent of the schoolteacher positions.

David S. Wyman
*The Abandonment of the
Jews*
1984

SWITZERLAND AND THE REFUGEES

The Swiss boat was not "overcrowded"; it was not "even full" and would have been able, even in politically stormy seas, to take on a far greater number of refugees without sinking.

Edgar Bonjour
History of Swiss Neutrality

Cited in Jewish Leadership During the Nazi Era, *edited by Randolph L. Braham, 1985.*

Abzug Commentary

As the first [newsreel] films of the liberated camps were shown, many people walked out of theaters all over England rather than witness the horrors. . . . At one cinema . . . British and other Allied soldiers blocked the exits and told the fleeing patrons . . . to see "what other people had to endure," to "go back and face it. . . ."

We must be our own soldiers, constantly on the lookout for subtle evasion. We must recognize that if we feel helpless when facing the record of human depravity, there was always a point at which any particular scene of madness could have been stopped.

Robert H. Abzug
Inside the Vicious Heart
1985

A Place for Holocaust Literature?

It would seem that a "Holocaust literature" is an impossibility—that, indeed, the phrase itself is a contradiction in terms. The reasons are at least threefold: first, there is no way to link a life-affirming enterprise such as literature with a death-bound phenomenon of such magnitude; second, no gift for literary description, no matter how blessed that gift, could possibly encompass the horror of Holocaust experience itself; third, since any writing involves some degree of distance, such "detachment" would violate the sanctity of the actual suffering and death undergone by the victims. . . .

And yet there is the fact of that literature itself to be

accounted for: Amidst the ruination of reason and meaning, that literature has been the most profound attempt, in our time, to find a meaning for the otherwise absurd, to find reason in what is otherwise inexplicable.

> Gila Ramras-Rauch
> Introduction to
> *Facing the Holocaust:*
>   *Selected Israeli Fiction,*
> edited by Gila
>   Ramras-Rauch and
>   Joseph Michman-
>   Melkman
> 1985

Abrams Commentary

What was it like to be a *mischling* [having one Jewish parent] in Nazi Germany? Or to be a Jew in a mixed marriage in a country officially without Jews? How did you feel when your Jewish parents, brothers, sisters, the lovers you might have married, your friends, neighbors, and even your schoolmates were all murdered—by the very people who chose to let *you* live? . . .

Those concepts of "right" and "wrong" lost their validity the day the Nazis killed their first Jew. Is it right to protect your spouse and your children? Is it wrong to save your own life? Or even to want to live? These are among the most basic of human concerns.

> Alan Abrams
> *Special Treatment*
> 1985

SHOULD WE BE REMINDED OF THE HOLOCAUST?

Is the Holocaust something we need to be reminded about annually or do you think after 40 years Jews should stop focusing on the Holocaust?

Should be reminded of the Holocaust . . . 46%
Jews should stop focusing on it . . . 40%

Roper Organization
Poll
1985

FIT TO PRINT?

Using space allotment and page placement as measures of importance, it is clear that even though much of this news [of events leading up to the Holocaust] came either from German sources or from eyewitness accounts, its relative news value was not always considered high. While certain reports were prominently placed in the major dailies, often news of significant value was relegated to the depths of the paper. *The New York Times* carried the reports of "massive arrests" of Jews in Vichy in a 26-line article on page 18 and the announcement that Jews over the age of six had to wear a star on page 14. The *New York Journal American* placed the announcement of German Jews' loss of all citizenship and residency rights and further confiscation of their property on page 30.

Deborah E. Lipstadt
Beyond Belief
1986

LIFTON COMMENTARY

I went to the [Auschwitz] camp a few years ago and was shown the many exhibits maintained there, exhibits that leave nothing to be added concerning the evil human beings can do to other human beings. But the one that left the most profound impression on me was the simplest of all: a room full of shoes, mostly baby shoes.

> Robert Jay Lifton
> *The Nazi Doctors*
> 1986

ON WINNING THE NOBEL PEACE PRIZE

I remember: it happened yesterday or eternities ago. A young Jewish boy discovered the kingdom of night. I remember his bewilderment. I remember his anguish. It all happened so fast. The ghetto. The deportation. The sealed cattle car. The fiery altar upon which the history of our people and the future of mankind were meant to be sacrificed. . . . And now the boy is turning to me: "What have you done with my future? What have you done with my life?"

And I tell him that I have tried. That I have tried to keep memory alive, that I have tried to fight those who would forget. Because if we forget, we are guilty. We are accomplices.

> Elie Wiesel
> Speech on accepting the
> Nobel Peace Prize
> Oslo, Norway
> December 10, 1986

FACKENHEIM COMMENTARY

Unlike the Turks, [in the Armenian killings] the Nazis sought a "final solution" of a "problem"—final only if, minimally, Europe and maximally, the world would be *judenrein* [Jew-free]. . . .

[The Jewish Holocaust] is without precedent and, thus far at least, without sequel. It is unique.

Equally unique are the means necessary to this end. These include (i) a scholastically precise definition of the victims; (ii) juridical procedures procuring their rightlessness; (iii) a technical apparatus culminating in murder trains and gas chambers; and (iv), most importantly, a veritable army of murderers and also direct and indirect accomplices: clerks, newspapermen, lawyers, bank managers, doctors, soldiers, railwaymen, entrepreneurs, and an endless list of others.

> Emil Fackenheim
> *The Jewish Thought of Emil Fackenheim: A Reader*
> Edited by Michael L. Morgan
> 1987

PORTRAIT OF A REVISIONIST

A new participant at the 1989 conference [of the Institute of Historical Review, a Holocaust revisionist group] was Fred Leuchter, Jr. Leuchter has described himself as the Chief Engineer of Fred Leuchter Associates in Boston, Massachusetts, and as an engineer specializing in gas chambers and executions and a consultant and engineer who specializes in the design and fabrication of execution hardware used in prisons throughout the United States. Leuchter has claimed that Auschwitz, Birkenau and Majdanek contained "no execution gas chambers" and "could not have been then, or now, be utilized or seriously considered to function as executing gas chambers."

> From *Holocaust*
> *Revisionism:*
> *Reinventing the Big Lie*
> Civil Rights Division
> Anti-Defamation League
> 1989

ON BEING GERMAN

It still isn't fun to be German. It's a bit like having a genetic disease for which a cure hasn't been found. Once in a while when a plucky New York cabdriver asks me, "Where are you from?" I snap back with a curt and icy "Why?"—as if revealing my nationality were an act of treason or could be used against me. History is a mean slasher. It lurks somewhere in the dark, crawls up to you surreptitiously, and lashes out. History hurts and haunts, leaving invisible scars, even on smooth, pink baby skin.

> Sabine Reichel
> *What Did You Do in the*
> *War, Daddy?*
> 1989

WIESEL COMMENTARY

God's silence allows evil, man's perversion engenders fear. Auschwitz did not descend from the heavens. Men conceived it, set it up, programmed it so as to assassinate other humans there. And they meant it to be for the well-being of humanity. And God let it happen. And humanity also. . . .

I shall live until the last day of my life without understanding.

Elie Wiesel
Living Philosophies, edited by
Clifton Fadiman
1990

"The Bloody Jews Again"

I asked one of my aunts once, and she gave a very one-sided account. She made the war sound heroic, and said everything we were taught about it was a lie. She had been there and knew more about it and said young people couldn't judge or criticize. In my family, they had always groaned, "Oh, not the bloody Jews again. They couldn't have killed that many, they are still everywhere—in the press, in industry, all over America."

Dagmar Drexel, daughter of
convicted war criminal
Max Drexel, describing
what relatives told her of
the war many years later

From Hitler's Children: Sons and Daughters of Leaders of the Third Reich Talk About Their Fathers and Themselves *by Gerald L. Posner, 1991.*

Mengele's Son Speaks

We, the children of these parents, we must deal with it. More than any other German group, up until now, we are faced with these issues. The other Germans say, "Okay, it happened, and it is too bad, but it's done and let's get on with life." They don't get involved as much as we, the children of the direct participants. I must always seem to have an answer for what he [Dr. Josef Mengele] did. He is gone, but he has left me here to answer the questions of what he did and why he did it. He is gone but I must bear the burden.

> Rolf Mengele
> *Hitler's Children: Sons and*
>   *Daughters of Leaders*
>   *of the Third Reich* by
> Gerald L. Posner
> 1991

KASTEN COMMENTARY

A large-scale rejection of the Hippocratic Oath and medical ethics occurred during the Third Reich, with flagrant abuses beginning in the 1930s after the passage of the 1933 Sterilization Law. In 1939, euthanasia was introduced as an instrument of state policy. Both decisions were associated with the new eugenics known as racial hygiene, which accompanied the rewriting of classic biology and Mendelian heredity by Nazi racial biologists. This led to organized murder of the handicapped and of mental patients in state institutions by psychiatrists and other medical personnel.

> Frederick H. Kasten
> Essay
> "Unethical Nazi Medicine in
> Annexed Alsace-Lorraine:
>   The Strange Case of Nazi
>   Anatomist Professor Dr.
>   August Hirt
> 1991

From Historians and Archivists: Essays in Modern German History and Archival Policy, *edited by George O. Kent.*

Katz Commentary

Post-1918 Europe was a breeding ground for conditions in which racial theory and political reality converged. The final coalescence of these two vectors after 1933 was neither "foreordained" nor "historically inevitable," but rather, one of the fecund possibilities that a traumatized and exhausted postwar Europe generated. The forces and personalities that could have acted to prevent this victory, that could have brought about some other scenario, failed the test, leaving Nazism, and its phantasmagoric racial doctrines, victorious.

Steven T. Katz
"1918 and After: The Role of
    Racial Anti-Semitism in the
    Nazi Analysis of the
    Weimar Republic"

From Anti-Semitism in Times of Crisis, edited by Sander L. Gilman and Steven T. Katz, 1991.

Gay Commentary

The remnant of Jews in Germany today is not a saving remnant but at best a fragile germ of a new community. Some 40,000 Jews live in the country now, but only a handful of them are German Jews. Most of them are the children and the grand-children of East European Jews who came out of the camps in 1945, sat on their suitcases for some years certain that they would never live in Germany, and then drifted into staying. A few, a very few, of the refugees who saved themselves from Hitler decided to return, and they are now dying out. Some of the old synagogues, torched in November 1938, have been restored and are in use, but they hear other melodies and see other observances. Like the Easter Island statues, they mutely evoke a past that is fast slipping from living memory, suggesting by their very scale a great culture that no longer exists. For that culture, along with its creators, fell victim to the Nazi regime and to the camps and, like the Yiddish-speaking culture of Eastern Europe, is little more than a memory.

Peter Gay
1992

From The Jews of Germany *by Ruth Gay.*

CARMICHAEL COMMENTARY

In the universe framed by Christian theology, the concepts of "Jews" and "Christians" have an undeniable balance that, while statistically absurd, reflects the fundamental theme of Christianity—the world of God and the world of the Devil. Since the Jews have not accepted the Christian God, they have ipso facto been arrayed alongside the Devil in Christendom. . . .

Jews have been called "Christ-killers," "enemies of God," "devils," "enemies of the human race." They have been considered utterly, eerily, and inhumanly Evil.

Joel Carmichael
The Satanization of the Jews
1992

OWINGS COMMENTARY

The concept of duty and following orders . . . was not limited to "Aryans." . . . Many sources confirm the hurt and bewilderment of Jewish Germans at suddenly being treated as if they were not regular upstanding citizens. How can anyone criticize them for not resisting the Nazis more? Apart from the near-futility of fighting a dictatorship from under its boot, had they not grown up, like other Germans, ready to trust the legendary governmental justice and to follow orders? And how could anyone wonder why so many stayed so long? . . . There was one main reason. Germany was home. They should leave their German language, landscape, and literature, not to mention Fatherland, not to mention work, because of some idiots now in power? . . . Jewish Germans rationalized, adjusted, hoped each new insult was the last, and waited for the return of their normal, orderly, German way of life.

> Alison Owings
> *Frauen: German Women
> Recall the Third Reich*
> 1993

DENIERS VS. REVISIONISTS

The deniers [of the Holocaust] consider themselves heirs of a group of influential American historians who were deeply disturbed by American involvement in World War I. These respected scholars, who called themselves revisionists, would have been appalled to learn of the purposes to which their arguments were put. In contrast to the Holocaust deniers, who make no distinction between fact and fiction, the World War I revisionists engaged in serious research and relied upon established canons of evidence. Despite these differences, deniers have tried to link the two traditions, arguing that each has sought to create an alternative history for major events of the 20th century. However, one of these schools used traditional historiographic methodology to do so, whereas denial relies on pseudoscience.

> Deborah E. Lipstadt
> *Denying the Holocaust*
> 1993

PERRY COMMENTARY

That many people, including intellectuals and members of the elites, believed these racial theories was an ominous sign for Western civilization. It showed how tenuous the rational tradition of the Enlightenment is, how receptive the mind is to dangerous myths, and how speedily human behavior can degenerate into inhumanity. Ending in the Holocaust, racist thinking constitutes a radical counter-ideology to the highest Western values, both Christian and humanist. For this reason, the Holocaust is the central event of the 20th century, or as a Jewish prayer expresses it: "Auschwitz is the fact and symbol of our era."

> Marvin Perry
> In the essay "Racial
>   Nationalism and the Rise
>   of Modern Anti-Semitism"
> *Jewish-Christian Encounters*
>   *Over the Centuries*, edited
>   by Marvin Perry and
>   Frederick Schweitzer
> 1994

BAUER COMMENTARY

The Nazi elite's decision to murder all Jews wherever they could reach them was implemented with thoroughness and conviction. But exceptions were granted during the war if tactical advantages could be gained by keeping some Jews alive or by letting some Jews escape to the free or neutral world. There was . . . no inherent contradiction between the two politics, one representing the main strategic line of Nazi thinking, and the other a tactical, secondary one. The Nazis expected to win the war, and if they did, they would finally "solve" the "Jewish question" by total annihilation; any Jews who might escape momentarily would in the end be caught and killed.

> Yehuda Bauer
> *Jews for Sale*
> 1994

FOGELMAN COMMENTARY

Fifty years ago, the wholesale slaughter of millions of people was unthinkable. It took the brutal inventiveness of Nazi Germany with its gas chambers, crematoriums, and methodical killing squads to show the modern world that when it comes to racial hatred, no cruelty is beyond the realm of possibility. In the final analysis, this was Hitler's most enduring and terrible legacy: after the Holocaust, no inhumanity is beyond imagining, no barbarity is inconceivable.

> Eva Fogelman
> *Conscience & Courage:*
> *Rescuers of Jews During the*
> *Holocaust*
> 1994

YAD VASHEM'S STANDARDS

Yad Vashem has honored more than 11,000 rescuers [of Jews during the Holocaust]. The criteria used by its awards commission to screen candidates are stringent and controversial. Only non-Jews are eligible, Jews who saved Jews are not recognized by Yad Vashem or anywhere else. To be considered for the honor, a person's deed must be above and beyond the simple offer of a helping hand. The good farmers who gave a bottle of milk and a loaf of bread to my father saved his life, but by Yad Vashem's standards, theirs was an ordinary act of charity.

Yad Vashem's recognition commission also screens out those who saved Jews for personal gain. These include people who were anxious to convert their charges to Christianity, people who wanted to adopt a child, and people who were paid or were promised payment in the future.

Eva Fogelman
Conscience & Courage:
Rescuers of Jews During
the Holocaust
1994

LUTHERAN STATEMENT

In the long history of Christianity there exists no more tragic development than the treatment accorded the Jewish people on the part of Christian believers. Very few Christian communities of faith were able to escape the contagion of anti-Judaism and its modern successor, anti-Semitism. Lutherans belonging to the Lutheran World Federation and the Evangelical Lutheran Church in America feel a special burden in this regard because of certain elements in the legacy of the reformer Martin Luther and the catastrophes, including the Holocaust of the twentieth century, suffered by Jews in places where the Lutheran churches were strongly represented.

The Lutheran communion of faith is linked by name and heritage to the memory of Martin Luther, teacher and reformer. Honoring his name in our own, we recall his bold stand for truth, his earthy and sublime words of wisdom, and above all his witness to God's saving word. Luther proclaimed a gospel for people as we really are, bidding us to trust a grace sufficient to reach our deepest shames and address the most tragic truths.

In the spirit of that truth-telling, we who bear his name and heritage must with pain acknowledge also Luther's anti-Judaic diatribes and violent recommendations of his later writings against the Jews. As did many of Luther's own companions in the sixteenth century, we reject this violent invective, and yet more do we express our deep and abiding sorrow over its tragic effects on subsequent generations. In concert with the Lutheran World Federation, we particularly deplore the appropriation of Luther's words by modern anti-Semites for the teaching of hatred toward Judaism or toward the Jewish people in our day.

Grieving the complicity of our own tradition within this history of hatred, moreover, we express our urgent desire to live out our faith in Jesus Christ with love and respect for the Jewish people. We recognize in anti-Semitism a contradiction and an affront to the Gospel, a violation of our hope and calling, and we pledge this church to oppose the deadly working of such bigotry, both within our own churches and in the society around us. Finally, we pray for the continued blessing of the Blessed One upon the increasing cooperation and understanding between Lutheran Christians and the Jewish community.

> Church Council of the
> Evangelical Lutheran
> Church in America
> Declaration
> April 18, 1994

LANGER COMMENTARY

I can hardly remember a Holocaust conference I've attended during the past decade where someone hasn't echoed George Santayana's solemn platitude that those who ignore the past are doomed to repeat it. The so-called ethnic cleansing in Yugoslavia is only one of a dozen episodes in recent years to prove that Santayana's maxim is nothing more than a piece of rhetorical excess—yet we continue to use it as if it played a vital role in defining the meaning of atrocity in our time. Indeed, it could be argued about the violence in Bosnia that the contending forces not only have *not* ignored the past of the Holocaust, but have paid careful attention *to* it in order to learn more about how to dehumanize their enemy in the name of some purifying ideology.

Lawrence L. Langer
Admitting the Holocaust:
Collected Essays
1995

NEW HOLOCAUST ARCHIVE

Destined to become the primary repository of Holocaust-related moving images in this country, the Steven Spielberg Film and Video Archive was established in October 1994. A generous gift from the Max Charitable Foundation, created by film producer Steven Spielberg, will allow the U.S. Holocaust Research Institute to expand its existing collection, and make it accessible to the public.

The first priority of the Spielberg archive is to acquire and organize all significant film and video images of the Holocaust and related aspects of World War II not yet in the Museum's collection. Archive staff members will search for materials in the major film repositories in Europe and the United States.

Eventually, the Spielberg archive will offer researchers unedited footage, military coverage, Nazi documentary and propaganda films, films taken by private individuals, censored war film footage, newsreels, and significant feature films and dramatic reconstructions.

U.S. Holocaust Memorial
Museum
The Year in Review,
1994–1995
1995

WEISS COMMENTARY

Despite a vast literature about anti-Semitism and the Holocaust, we do not yet understand why the destruction of the Jews was conceived and implemented by the Germans. . . . Only among the Germans did racist stereotypes evolve into a popular mandated ideology of such lethal force as to end in the horror of the death camps. To understand this, the most important and difficult historical question of our time, it is necessary to explore the special nature of German and Austrian history, for therein lies the key to the immense power of anti-Semitism among millions of Germans and the reasons why, long before the Nazis, the historical basis of their success was built.

. . . Today most historians believe that the Nazis had no deep roots in German history, that anti-Semitism in Germany was not essentially different from that of some other nations. . . . Some have even claimed, "No Hitler, no Holocaust."

I believe these views to be incorrect. . . .

John Weiss
Ideology of Death: Why the Holocaust Happened in Germany
1996

Epilogue

In a dreadful moment in history it was argued that one only carried out unjust laws in order to weaken them severely, that the power one agreed to exercise would have done even more damage if it had been placed in hands which were less pure. What a deceitful rationalization, which opened the door to unlimited criminality! Everyone eased his conscience, and each level of injustice found a willing executor. In such circumstances, it seems to me, innocence was murdered, with the pretext that it be strangled more gently.

Benjamin Constant
1815

Cited in Vichy France and the Jews *by Michael R. Marrus and Robert O. Paxton.*

Who's Who

Alan Abrams is a Canadian author and journalist.

Robert H. Abzug is an author and professor of history.

R. Solomon ibn Lahmish Alami wrote about problems of Spanish Jews during the 14th and 15th centuries.

Ruth Andreas-Friedrich has written of the desperate attempts by Jews to escape from Nazi Germany.

Hannah Arendt was born in Germany. When Hitler came to power, she fled first to France and later to the United States. She wrote *Eichmann in Jerusalem.*

Mikhail Bakunin was a Russian-born anarchist of the 19th century.

Arthur J. Balfour, British Foreign Secretary during the First World War, issued the declaration of Jewish nationhood which bears his name.

Dr. Sola Baron is a Jewish historian and scholar.

Elvira Bauer was the author of record of an anti-Semitic book published by Julius Streicher. It was introduced into evidence at Nuremberg.

Yehuda Bauer is Professor of Holocaust Studies at Hebrew University, Jerusalem.

Dr. August Becker was identified at Nuremberg as the man who constructed the vans used to gas Jews. They would be led into the van, the motor would be turned on, and the exhaust fumes would be released inside the van.

David Ben-Gurion, originally born in Poland, came to Palestine as a young man. It was then part of the Ottoman Empire. During World War I, he was expelled from Palestine, but returned after the war. A prominent Zionist leader, he later became first Prime Minister of the new state of Israel.

Martin S. Bergmann has studied and written about the effects of the Holocaust on the second generation.

Peter Bergson was a Jew from the British Mandate of Palestine. Head of the Committee for a Jewish Army, he sought support in the United States for the rescue of European Jewry. His real name was Hillel Kook, nephew of the late Chief Rabbi Abraham Isaac Kook. Bergson, a member of the Irgun, took the pseudonym because he did not want his politics to impact on his family.

Karl Ludwig Borne was a German Jew born toward the end of the 18th century. He converted to Christianity in order to advance his career, but regretted it later.

Czeslaw Borowi was born in Treblinka and lived there all his life. He was interviewed for the motion picture, *Shoah*. The interviews were later published in book form.

Viktor Brack, who had been running a euthanasia program in Nazi Germany, was asked to turn his personnel over for a new "euthanasia" program.

Milton Bracker was a reporter for the *New York Times*.

Edgar Bonjour, Swiss historian, has written on the history of Swiss neutrality.

Monsignor Giuseppe Burzio was the Vatican's Charge d'Affaires in Bratislava during the war.

Harry C. Butcher was an aide to General Eisenhower during World War II.

Arthur R. Butz has written a book denying the Holocaust, referring to it as a hoax.

Joel Carmichael has written extensively on Russia and the Soviet Union. He has also written several books on Christianity.

Houston Stewart Chamberlain was an Englishman so fond of

Germany that he changed his citizenship. He married Richard Wagner's daughter.

Neville Chamberlain was British Prime Minister in the late 1930s. He pursued a policy of appeasing Hitler until the invasion of Poland in 1939. He resigned in 1940, just before the fall of France.

Winston Churchill succeeded Neville Chamberlain as Prime Minister of the United Kingdom in 1940.

Benjamin Constant was a Swiss-born French politician and journalist. His career bridged the 18th and 19th centuries.

Eugene Davidson is the author of *The Trial of the Germans*.

Lucy S. Dawidowicz was one of the foremost scholars of the Holocaust.

Hans Heinrich Dieckhoff was the German ambassador to the United States at the time of the 1938 German pogroms.

Dagmar Drexel is the daughter of Max Drexel. He spent several years in prison as a war criminal.

Adolf Eichmann was head of the Jewish Office of the Gestapo. After the war, he escaped to South America, was brought back to Israel to stand trial and was hanged.

Dwight Eisenhower, Supreme Commander of all Allied forces in Europe, later became President of the United States.

Howard Elting, Jr., was U.S. Vice Consul in Geneva Switzerland, during World War II.

Bernt Engelmann was imprisoned in Dachau for opposing the Nazi regime. After the war, he became a journalist, writing and editing for *Der Spiegel* and other publications.

Pope Eugenius IV held the post during the middle of the 15th century.

Emil Fackenheim, a German Jewish philosopher, was an inmate at Sachsenhausen concentration camp. He has written numerous books and articles. A former Professor of Philosophy at the University of Toronto, he has been a Fellow at the Institute of Contemporary Jewry at Hebrew University, Jerusalem.

Konnilyn G. Feig, both a teacher and student of the Holocaust, has developed courses of study on the subject. She is the author of *Hitler's Death Camps*.

Fania Fenelon, a French Jew, played in the all-women's orchestra at Birkenau. She survived the war, and her story was dramatized on television.

Joachim C. Fest, a German journalist, has served on the editorial board of the *Frankfurter Allgemeine Zeitung.*

Fritz Fink, a municipal school inspector during the Third Reich, wrote an anti-Semitic pamphlet for *Der Stuermer.*

Ludwig Fischer was in charge of the Warsaw district for the Nazis. His order established the Warsaw Ghetto.

Harold Flender has written of the Danish rescue of Jews and presented a television documentary on the subject.

Moses Flinker kept a diary during the Nazi occupation of Belgium.

Eva Fogelman, a psychotherapist, is a founding director of the Jewish Foundation for Christian Rescuers.

Frank Foley was the British Passport Control Officer serving in Berlin in 1935.

Henry Ford, founder of the automobile company, published the anti-Semitic *Dearborn Independent.* He later apologized for having done so.

Anne Frank hid with her family in an Amsterdam attic until they were discovered by the Nazis. She died at Bergen-Belsen. Her diary became world-famous.

Hans Frank was the Nazi governor-general of Poland. A defendant at Nuremberg, he was found guilty of crimes against humanity and was hanged.

Ellen Frey was born in Germany before Hitler came to power and was part of the German community during the Third Reich.

Hans Fritzsche was head of the radio division of the Nazi Propaganda Ministry. He was tried at Nuremberg and was acquitted.

Peter Gay wrote the introduction to Ruth Gay's *The Jews of Germany.*

Kurt Gerstein, chief disinfection officer of the Waffen SS, handled the disinfection of clothes left behind by Jews in the death camps.

Misha Gildenman was a Jewish Partisan who fought the Nazis in the forests of the Ukraine. He is said to have begun with ten men and a single knife—and built up a heavily-armed force in the hundreds.

Odilo Globocnik organized the "Operation Reinhard" project for Heinrich Himmler. It involved the planning, construction, and operation of death camps for the Final Solution. He committed suicide after the war.

Joseph Goebbels was Hitler's minister of propaganda. He committed suicide during the last days of the war in Europe.

Edda Goering was the only child of Hermann Goering.

Hermann Goering, an early Hitler crony, was in charge of the Luftwaffe, the German Air Force. Sentenced to death at Nuremberg, he took poison hours before he was to be hanged.

Arthur J. Goldberg, former Associate Justice of the U.S. Supreme Court, served as head of the American Jewish Commission on the Holocaust in the early 1980s.

Werner Goldberg was a *mischling* in Nazi Germany, so called because one of his parents was Jewish. He served in the Wehrmacht, and, according to author Alan Abrams, the Propaganda Ministry once singled him out as "the perfect Aryan soldier."

Hermann Graebe, a German civilian, worked as a construction engineer during the war. His sworn affidavit was introduced into testimony at Nuremberg during the war crimes trials.

Hayim Greenberg, a Labor Zionist, tried to arouse the American Jewish community to the plight of European Jewry.

Hana Greenfield, born in Czechoslovakia, was imprisoned in several concentration camps. She survived the war and made her home in Israel.

Saint Gregory of Nyssa was a Church theologian of the 4th century.

Sally Grubman, a Polish Jew, survived both Auschwitz and Ravensbruck. In the latter camp, she was part of a Nazi medical experiment.

Warden Gunther was in charge of the Nazi prison at Minsk.

John H. Hanson is an English professor at Virginia Commonwealth University.

Leslie Hardman was a Jewish chaplain with the British Army when it liberated Bergen-Belsen.

Ben Hecht, a novelist and screenwriter, wrote many articles, newspaper ads, and dramatic presentations on behalf of European Jewry. He worked closely with Peter Bergson.

Heinrich Heine was a German Jewish poet, born at the end of the 18th century. Baptized, he found himself scorned by both Jews and Christians.

Adolph Held represented the Jewish Labor Committee at a meeting between Jewish leaders and President Roosevelt in December 1942.

Commandant Hubert Henry was a French Army intelligence officer. He was a key witness at the court-martial of Captain Alfred Dreyfus, who was charged with spying for Germany. Henry later confessed to forging documents to frame Dreyfus and died in prison under mysterious circumstances.

Herman Herskocic, a Czech Jew, tried to get to Palestine during World War II. His trip was a true odyssey of adventure and misadventure. He ended up in the Czech Free Army, interrogating German prisoners-of-war.

Rabbi Arthur Hertzberg was a member of the American Jewish Commission on the Holocaust in the early 1980s.

Theodor Herzl, born in Hungary, was a journalist who became father of the modern Zionist movement.

Reinhard Heydrich was originally put in charge of Hitler's Final Solution to slaughter the Jews of Europe. He was assassinated.

Hillel was a Jewish scholar of the first century, B.C.E.

Heinrich Himmler, head of the Nazi SS, was in charge of carrying out Hitler's plan to annihilate the European Jews. Caught by the British at the end of the war, he committed suicide.

Adolf Hitler was the leader of the Nazi party which took power in Germany in 1933. His racial policies led to the slaughter of six million Jews and millions of others during World War II. He committed suicide in a Berlin bunker in 1945.

Rudolf Hoess, commandant at Auschwitz, was put on trial after the war and executed.

Wilhelm Hoettl was Deputy Group Leader of the Foreign Office Section of the Nazi Security Section. He was given the count of six million Jewish dead by Adolf Eichmann, himself.

Heinz Hohne has written the history of the SS, *The Order of the Death's Head.*

Pope Innocent III headed the Catholic Church from 1198–

1216. At the fourth Lateran Council, in 1215, major anti-Jewish restrictions were enacted. It was at this council that the Jewish Badge was introduced.

Vladimir Jabotinsky, born in Russia, was a writer and Zionist leader. He organized self-defense forces in Palestine after World War I and is regarded as the spiritual father of the Irgun.

Chaim A. Kaplan kept a diary in the Warsaw Ghetto. It was published after the war.

Marion A. Kaplan, Associate Professor of History at Queens College and the Graduate Center, City University of New York, has written a number of books on German history and women's history.

Jan Karski was a member of the Polish Underground, reporting directly to the Polish Government-in-exile.

Frederick H. Kasten, now retired, was a professor in the Department of Anatomy, Louisiana State University, New Orleans.

Steven T. Katz is Professor of Near Eastern Studies and Jewish Studies at Cornell University.

Itzhak Katzenelson was a Hebrew poet and playwright who lived and worked in Lodz, Poland. He died at Auschwitz.

Ka-tzetnik 135633 is the pseudonym of a novelist and poet who has written about the Holocaust. Her novel, *House of Dolls,* is about a Nazi brothel; *Star Eternal* is a collection of poetry.

Lt. General Katzmann headed a German police unit in Poland.

Fritz Klein was a doctor at Auschwitz.

H. R. Knickerbocker, a reporter for the *New York Evening Post,* was thrown out of Nazi Germany for writing news stories the Nazis didn't like.

Eugen Kogon is the author of the classic *The Theory and Practice of Hell.*

Shalom Kohn, a Polish Jew, was a leader of the Treblinka uprising of 1943. He was one of a handful of survivors.

Janusz Korczak, a Polish Jew, was a writer and educator. In charge of a Jewish orphanage in the Warsaw ghetto, he insisted on accompanying the children when they were shipped to Treblinka.

Vladimir Korolenko was a Russian journalist who covered the Beilis trial.

Josef Kramer, commandant of several Nazi concentration camps, was tried for war crimes and executed.

Rita Kuhn, half-Jewish, was born in Germany and lived there during the war years.

Paul de Lagarde was a 19th century German scholar.

Fiorello H. LaGuardia, a former Congressman, was mayor of New York City throughout the war.

Lawrence L. Langer, a U.S. Senator from North Dakota and Holocaust scholar, won the 1991 National Book Critics Circle Award for criticism.

William Langer was the U.S. Senator from North Dakota.

Bill Lawrence was a war correspondent for the *New York Times*.

Simone Legrange was caught up in the Nazi net in France. Her mother and father were killed at Auschwitz. Simone lived to testify against Klaus Barbie, her oppressor.

Max Lerner was a columnist and editorial writer for the newspaper *PM*.

John L. Lewis, head of the United Mine Workers, was a top leader of the CIO until the U.M.W. disaffiliated.

Robert Ley was in charge of Hitler's Labor Office. He ran the slave labor program during the war. Charged at Nuremberg, he committed suicide before the trial ended.

Bernhard Lichtenberg was Dean of the Cathedral of St. Hedwig in Berlin. He denounced attacks on the Jews as un-Christian, served two years in prison, and died on his way to a concentration camp.

Robert Jay Lifton, a distinguished psychiatrist, has written extensively on the role that German doctors played in Nazi genocide.

Walter Lippmann was regarded as one of America's most distinguished political analysts.

Anne Morrow Lindbergh, the poetess, was the wife of Charles A. Lindbergh.

Charles A. Lindbergh was the first aviator to fly alone across the Atlantic. He was a prominent isolationist, opposing America's entry into World War II.

Albert S. Lindemann is the author of *The Jew Accused.*

Deborah E. Lipstadt holds the Dorot Chair in Modern Jewish and Holocaust Studies at Emory University, Atlanta. She has written books on Holocaust deniers and on the American press during the Holocaust period.

William B. Lovelady was an officer of the U.S. Third Armored Division, which liberated the Nordhausen concentration camp in 1945.

Stefan Lux, a German Jew barred from making films in Nazi Germany, committed suicide at the League of Nations in 1936.

Dwight Macdonald was a political essayist.

Cardinal Maglione served as Secretary of State in the Vatican.

Ber Mark, a historian of the Holocaust, directed the Jewish Historical Institute of Warsaw.

Thomas Mann was a German novelist.

Michael R. Marrus, professor of modern European history at the University of Toronto, is coauthor of *Vichy France and the Jews.*

Karl Marx was a 19th century journalist and political philosopher. The father of Communism was born a German Jew, but was baptized at six. Many of his writings displayed virulent anti-Semitism.

Matthew was one of the apostles of Jesus. He was also one of four evangelists who preached the gospel.

Sigmund Mazur was a lab assistant who worked at the Danzig Anatomic Institute on experiments to make soap from dead Jews.

Vladka Meed acted as a courier between the Jewish fighters inside the Warsaw ghetto and supporters outside the ghetto walls. She survived the war and came to America.

Rolf Mengele is son of Dr. Josef Mengele, the notorious Nazi doctor of Auschwitz. Rolf was born a year before the end of the war. His father fled to South America to escape trial. There he lived in hiding until his death. Rolf has changed his name.

Eric Mills was the Commissioner for Migration and Statistics in Palestine in 1935.

Henry Monsky represented B'nai B'rith at a meeting between Jewish leaders and President Roosevelt in December 1942.

Leland Morris was attached to the U.S. embassy in Berlin.

Lord Moyne was the top British official in the Middle East at the time of the Nazi proposal to swap Hungarian Jews for trucks. Moyne, decidedly cool to the idea of taking Jews into Palestine, was assassinated by Jewish extremists.

Edward R. Murrow, a radio reporter during the war, later became the pre-eminent television journalist.

Rev. Martin Niemoeller, a Protestant minister, publicly opposed the Nazis. He was imprisoned from 1937 until the end of the war.

Ivar C. Olsen, representing the U.S. War Refugee Board in Sweden, approved the selection of Raoul Wallenberg on the mission to save Hungarian Jews.

Caliph Omar II built a mosque in Jerusalem in the seventh century. It was later replaced by a more permanent structure, the Mosque of Omar, also known as the Dome of the Rock.

Alison Owings is a freelance television news writer.

Blaise Pascal was a 17th century French philosopher and mathematician.

Robert O. Paxton, professor of modern Western European history at Columbia University, is coauthor of *Vichy France and the Jews.*

Alexander Pechersky, a Russian Jew, was brought to Sobibor as a prisoner-of-war. He led a large-scale rebellion in Sobibor and escaped to fight again.

Frances Perkins was Secretary of Labor in Franklin Roosevelt's administration.

Dr. Pernutz was prefect of the Tarnow District, Poland.

Marvin Perry is an associate professor of history at Baruch College, City University of New York.

Pope Pius XI, who headed the Catholic Church from 1922 to 1939, was an outspoken foe of Nazi racial policies. In 1938, he had assigned the drafting of an encyclical condemning both racism and anti-Semitism, but he died before it could be promulgated.

Pope Pius XII was leader of the Catholic Church during World War II. There is still great controversy among the scholars over whether or not the Pope could have done more to help Jews during the Holocaust.

Ezra Pound, American poet and essayist, made propaganda broadcasts from Rome during World War II. Brought up on treason charges after the war, he was found to be insane.

Marion Pritchard saved Jews in Holland during the Holocaust. She is now a psychoanalyst, living in Vermont.

Pierre-Joseph Proudhon was a French anarchist of the 19th century.

Franz Rademacher worked for the Nazi Foreign Ministry. He proposed a plan to resettle European Jews on the island of Madagascar, off the eastern coast of Africa.

Gila Ramras-Rauch, born in Tel Aviv, is an author and educator.

Gustav Ratzenhofer was an Austrian sociologist during the 19th and early 20th centuries.

Sabine Reichel is a German-born writer who now lives in the United States.

Emmanuel Ringelblum was a historian who kept careful notes and assembled documentation on life in the Warsaw ghetto.

Ernst Roehm headed the SA, the Nazi Party's private army. He was murdered on Hitler's orders in the blood purge of 1934.

Franklin D. Roosevelt, who won election as President an unprecedented four times, backed aid for Britain before the United States officially entered the war. He died shortly before the end of World War II. His action—and inaction—to save the Jews of Europe remain a major debate among historians and biographers.

Theodore Roosevelt was Police Commissioner of New York City, Assistant Secretary of the Navy, and Vice President. He became President on the assassination of William McKinley.

Alfred Rosenberg, born in Estonia, came to Germany after World War I. He became a confidant of Hitler. In July of 1941 he was named Reich Minister for the Eastern Occupied Territories. He was later found guilty of war crimes and crimes against humanity and was hanged at Nuremberg.

Rabbi Israel Rosenberg represented the Union of Orthodox Rabbis at a meeting between President Roosevelt and Jewish leaders in December 1942.

Sylvia Rothchild edited the memoirs which were published in *Voices from the Holocaust.*

Gerd von Rundstedt was a German Field Marshal who led armies into Poland, France, and the Soviet Union.

Solomon Schechter, a distinguished Jewish scholar, was born in Rumania. He emigrated first to England and then to the United States. He founded the Conservative Jewish movement.

Baldur von Schirach was head of the Hitler Youth. He was tried at Nuremberg and sentenced to 20 years imprisonment.

Harold M. Schulweiss was the California rabbi who came up with the idea of honoring Christians who risked their lives to save Jews during the Holocaust.

William L. Shirer was the CBS radio news correspondent who wrote *Berlin Diary* and the classic *Rise and Fall of the Third Reich.*

Lt.-Col. Truman Smith was U.S. Military Attache in Berlin during the middle to late 1930s. His reports appear to show a favorable attitude toward Nazi Germany.

Albert Speer, Hitler's architect, became Minister of Armaments during World War II. Because of his involvement in the slave labor program, he was found guilty of war crimes at Nuremberg. He served 20 years in prison.

SS Brigade Fuehrer Stahlecker was in charge of Action Group A in the Baltics. His own group—and partisan groups he encouraged—murdered 135,000 persons, mostly Jews.

Marshal Joseph Stalin, Soviet dictator, made a pact with Hitler in which they divided Poland. Two years later, Hitler attacked the Soviet Union.

Dr. Leo Stein wrote of concentration camp experiences at Sachsenhausen.

Julius Streicher tried to start his own anti-Semitic party before joining the Nazis in 1921. In 1922, he started *Der Stuermer,* a virulently anti-Semitic and pornographic publication. He was hanged at Nuremberg for crimes against humanity.

General Juergen Stroop was the Nazi officer in charge of deporting the last Jews from the Warsaw ghetto. It took him a month to crush the last resistance.

Arthur Szyk was an artist and muralist. He created many anti-Nazi drawings.

Edmond Taylor was the correspondent for the *Chicago Tribune* when the Nazis came to power in Germany. He was expelled by the authorities who did not like what he was writing.

Myron Taylor was President Roosevelt's personal representative to the Vatican.

Dorothy Thompson was a newspaper columnist and radio commentator.

Harold H. Tittmann served as assistant to Myron Taylor.

Leo Tolstoy was a Russian novelist.

Mark Twain was an American novelist and essayist.

Gabor Vajna was Minister of the Interior for the Hungarian puppet government set up by the Nazis in the fall of 1944.

Xavier Vallat was chosen to head the Commissariat for Jewish Questions by the Vichy French government. A notorious anti-Semite, he instituted major anti-Jewish measures and faced collaboration charges at the end of the war.

Pierre Van Paassen was a journalist and author.

Masimo Adolfo Vitale, an Italian Jew, has written extensively on Italian history.

Rudolf Vrba, a Slovak Jew, escaped from Auschwitz in April 1944. He and Alfred Wetzler brought word to the outside world of what was happening there.

Robert G. L. Waite is the author of *The Psychopathic God: Adolf Hitler.*

Raoul Wallenberg was a Swedish diplomat who worked with the U.S. War Refugee Board. He saved thousands of Hungarian Jews by giving them Swedish passports. After Budapest fell to the Russian Army, he was arrested by Soviet authorities. His fate is unknown.

Tom Watson was a Georgia populist. His anti-Semitic attacks during the Leo Frank case led to Watson's election to the U.S. Senate.

John Weiss is a professor of history at Lehman College and the Graduate Center of the City University of New York.

Chaim Weizmann, born in Poland, became director of the British Admiralty Chemical Laboratories. An ardent Zionist, he attempted to help the victims of Nazi persecution during World War II. He became first president of the state of Israel.

Leon W. Wells, a concentration camp survivor, testified against Nazi war criminals.

Maurice Wertheim represented the American Jewish Committee at a meeting between President Roosevelt and Jewish leaders in December 1942.

Alfred Wetzler was a Slovak Jew who escaped from Auschwitz.

T. W. White represented Australia at the Evian conference.

Elie Wiesel, a survivor of the Holocaust, wrote a number of books on the subject. He won the Nobel Peace Prize in 1986.

Simon Wiesenthal survived a number of concentration camps to become the great Nazi-hunter after the war.

Rev. Gerald B. Winrod spread anti-Semitic messages throughout the United States during the 1930s and 1940s.

Eduard Wirths was the garrison physician at Auschwitz.

Rabbi Stephen Wise was an outspoken advocate of liberal issues. He founded the American Jewish Congress and the Jewish Institute of Religion. A prominent Zionist, he was a friend of Presidents Woodrow Wilson and Franklin Roosevelt. In December 1942, he led a delegation of Jewish leaders to ask Roosevelt to act on behalf of European Jewry.

Foreign Minister Witting was a major figure in the Finnish government during World War II.

Karl Wolff was an SS official at Treblinka.

Michael Wolffsohn is Professor of Government at the University of the Bundesstaat in Germany.

David S. Wyman is a professor of history at the University of Massachusetts, Amherst. He wrote *The Abandonment of the Jews.*

Israel Zangwill, an English Jewish writer, was best known for his descriptions of Jewish life.

Szmul Zygielbojm, Bund representative with the Polish Council in Exile, committed suicide in 1943. He was protesting the inaction of Allied governments to save the Jews of Europe.

Bibliography

Abrams, Alan. *Special Treatment: The Untold Story of Hitler's Third Race.* Secaucus, N.J.: Lyle Stuart, 1985.

Abzug, Robert H. *Inside the Vicious Heart: Americans and the Liberation of Nazi Concentration Camps.* New York: Oxford University Press, 1985.

American Jewish Committee. *The Jews in Nazi Germany: The Factual Record of Their Persecution by the National Socialists.* New York: 1933.

Andreas-Friedrich, Ruth. *Berlin Underground.* Latimer House, 1948.

Arad, Yitzhak. *Belzec, Sobibor, Treblinka: The Operation Reinhard Death Camps.* Bloomington, IN: Indiana University Press, 1987.

Arad, Yitzhak, Israel Gutman, and Abraham Margaliot, eds. *Documents on the Holocaust.* Jerusalem: Yad Vashem, 1981.

Arendt, Hannah. *Eichmann in Jerusalem: The Banality of Evil.* New York: Viking Press, 1963.

Baron, Joseph L., editor. *A Treasury of Jewish Quotations.* New York: Crown, 1956.

Bauer, Yehuda. *Jews for Sale: Nazi-Jewish Negotiations, 1933–1945.* New Haven, CT: Yale University Press, 1994.

Baynes, Norman H., ed. *The Speeches of Adolf Hitler.* London, 1942.

Ben-Sasson, H. H., ed. *History of the Jewish People.* Cambridge, MA: Harvard University Press, 1976.

Bierman, John. *Righteous Gentile: The Story of Raoul Wallenberg.* New York: Viking, 1981.

Boelcke, Willi A., ed. *The Secret Conferences of Dr. Goebbels: The Nazi Propaganda War 1939–43.* Translated from the German by Edward Oseres. New York: E. P. Dutton, 1970.

Bower, Tom. *Klaus Barbie: The Butcher of Lyons.* New York: Pantheon, 1984.

Braham, Randolph L., ed. *Jewish Leadership During the Nazi Era: Patterns of Behavior in the Free World.* New York: Columbia University Press, 1985.

Bureau of Curriculum Development. *Teaching About the Holocaust and Genocide*, The Human Rights Series, Vol. II. Albany, NY: State Education Department, 1985.

Butcher, Harry C. *My Three Years with Eisenhower.* New York: Simon & Schuster, 1946.

Butz, Arthur R. *The Hoax of the 20th Century.* Torrance, CA: Institute for Historical Review, 1976.

Carmichael, Joel. *The Satanization of the Jews: Origin and Development of Mystical Anti-Semitism.* New York: Fromm International, 1992.

Civil Rights Division. *Holocaust Revisionism: Reinventing the Big Lie.* New York: Anti-Defamation League, 1989.

Cohen, Susan Blacher, ed. *From Hester Street to Hollywood: The Jewish-American Stage and Screen.* Bloomington, IN: Indiana University Press, 1983.

Cohn, Norman. *Warrant for Genocide: The Myth of the Jewish World-wide Conspiracy and the Protocols of the Elders of Zion.* Chico, CA: Scholars Press, 1981.

Davidson, Eugene. *The Trial of the Germans: An Account of the 22 Defendants before the International Military Tribunal at Nuremberg.* New York: Macmillan, 1966.

Dawidowicz, Lucy S. *The Holocaust and the Historians.* Cambridge, MA: Harvard University Press, 1981.

Dawidowicz, Lucy S., ed. *The Holocaust Reader.* New York: Behrman House, 1976.

Dawidowicz, Lucy S. *The War Against the Jews 1933–1945*. New York: Holt, Rinehart & Winston, 1975.

Dodd, William E., Jr., and Martha Dodd, eds. *Ambassador Dodd's Diary, 1933–1938*. Gollancz, 1941.

Donat, Alexander, ed. *The Death Camp Treblinka: A Documentary*. New York: Holocaust Library, 1979.

Doob, Leonard, ed. *Ezra Pound Speaking*. Westport, CT: Greenwood Press, 1978.

Duker, Abraham. *Jewish Survival in the World Today*. New York: Hadassah, 1940.

Dundes, Alan, ed. *The Blood Libel Legend: A Casebook in Anti-Semitic Folklore*. Madison, WI: University of Wisconsin Press, 1991.

Eisenberg, Azriel, compiler. *Eyewitnesses to Jewish History, 586 B.C.E.–1967*. New York: Union of American Hebrew Congregations, 1973.

Engelmann, Bernt. *In Hitler's Germany: Daily Life in the Third Reich*. Translated from the German by Krishna Winston. New York: Random House, 1986.

Fadiman, Clifton, ed. *Living Philosophies*. Wiesel segment translated by Martha Liptzin Hauptman. New York: Doubleday, 1990.

Feig, Konnilyn G. *Hitler's Death Camps: The Sanity of Madness*. London: Holmes & Meier, 1979.

Fenelon, Fania, with Marcelle Routier. *Playing for Time*. Translated from the French by Judith Landry. New York: Atheneum, 1977.

Fest, Joachim C. *Hitler*. New York: Harcourt Brace Jovanovich, 1974. Translated from the German by Richard and Clara Winston. Verlag Ullstein edition, 1973.

Flender, Harold. *Rescue in Denmark*. New York: Holocaust Library, 1963.

Flinker, Moses. *The Lad Moses: The Diary of Moses Flinker*. Jerusalem: Yad Vashem, [n.d.].

Fogelman, Eva. *Conscience and Courage: Rescuers of Jews During the Holocaust*. New York: Doubleday, 1994.

Frank, Anne. *The Diary of a Young Girl*. New York: Doubleday, 1952.

Fred R. Crawford Witness to the Holocaust Project. Atlanta: Emory University.

Friedman, Philip. *Their Brothers' Keepers*. New York: Holocaust Library, 1963.

Furman, Harry, ed. *Holocaust and Genocide*. State of New Jersey Department of Education. New York: Anti-Defamation League, 1983.

Gay, Ruth. *The Jews of Germany: A Historical Portrait*. New Haven: Yale University Press, 1992.

Gilbert, Martin. *The Holocaust: A History of the Jews of Europe During the Second World War*. New York: Holt, Rinehart & Winston, 1985.

Gildenman, Misha. *The Destruction of Koretz*. Paris, [n.p.], 1949.

Gilman, Sander L., and Steven T. Katz. *Anti-Semitism in Times of Crisis*. New York: New York University Press, 1991.

Glock, Charles Y., and Rodney Stark. *Christian Beliefs and Anti-Semitism*. New York: Harper & Row, 1966.

Golden, Harry. *A Little Girl is Dead*. Cleveland: World Publishing Co., 1965.

Gould, Allan, collector and ed. *What Did They Think About the Jews?*. Northvale, NJ: Jason Aronson Inc., 1991.

Greenfield, Hana. *Fragments of Memory*. Jerusalem: Gefen, 1992.

Gutman, Israel, editor-in-chief. *Encyclopedia of the Holocaust*. New York: Macmillan, 1990.

Hardman, Leslie. *The Survivors*. London: Vallentine Mitchell, 1958.

Hecht, Ben. *A Child of the Century*. New York: Simon & Schuster, 1954.

Herzl, Theodor. *The Jewish State*, 1896.

Hilberg, Raul. *The Destruction of the European Jews*. New York: Harper & Row, 1961.

Hirschler, Gertrude, ed. *Ashkenaz: The German Jewish Heritage*. Based on museum exhibition. New York: Yeshiva University Museum, 1988.

Hitler, Adolf. *Mein Kampf*. Original German publication 1925. London: Hutchinson Publishing, Ltd., 1969.

Hohne, Heinz. *The Order of the Death's Head*. Hamburg: Verlag der Spiegel, 1966. Translated from the German by Richard Barry. New York: Coward-McCann, 1970.

International Military Tribunal. *Nazi Conspiracy and Aggres-*

sion. Washington, D.C.: U.S. Government Printing Office, 1946.

Jabotinsky, Vladimir. *The Jewish War Front*. London: Allen & Unwin, 1940.

Watson, Tom. Editorial in *Jeffersonian*. Thomson, GA. (August, 1915).

Kaplan, Chaim A. *Scroll of Agony: Warsaw Ghetto Diary*. Translated by Abraham I. Katsh. New York: Collier Books, 1973.

Kaplan, Marion A. *The Making of the Jewish Middle Class: Women, Family, and Identity in Imperial Germany*. New York: Oxford University Press, 1991.

Karski, Jan. *Story of a Secret State*. 1944.

Ka-tzetnik 135633. *Star Eternal*. Originally published in Hebrew under the title, *Star of Ashes*, by Mossad Bialik, Ltd. New York: Arbor House, 1971.

Kendrick, Alexander. *Prime Time: The Life of Edward R. Murrow*. Boston: Little, Brown and Co., 1969.

Kent, George O., ed. *Historians and Archivists: Essays in Modern German History and Archival Policy*. Fairfax, VA: George Mason University Press, 1991.

Kogon, Eugen. *The Theory and Practice of Hell*. New York: Berkeley, 1950.

Korczak, Janusz. *Ghetto Diary*. Translated from Polish by Jerzy Bachrach and Barbara Krzywicka (Vedder). New York: Holocaust Library, 1978.

Korman, Gerd. *Hunter and the Hunted*. New York: Viking, 1973.

Landstrom, Russell. *Associated Press News Annual, 1945*. New York: Rinehart & Co., 1946.

Langer, Lawrence L. *Admitting the Holocaust: Collected Essays*. New York: Oxford University Press, 1995.

Langer, Lawrence L. *The Holocaust and the Literary Imagination*. New Haven: Yale University Press, 1975.

Lanzmann, Claude. *Shoah: An Oral History of the Holocaust*. The complete text of the film. New York: Pantheon, 1985. Originally published in France by Librairie Artheme Fayard.

Laqueur, Walter, and Barry Rubin, eds. *The Israel-Arab Reader: A Documentary History of the Middle East Conflict*. 4th rev. ed. New York: Viking Penguin, 1984.

Lee, A. *Henry Ford and the Jews*. New York: Stein & Day, 1980.

Lester, Elenore. *Wallenberg: The Man in the Iron Web*. Englewood Cliffs, N.J.: Prentice-Hall, 1982.

Lifton, Robert Jay. *The Nazi Doctors: Medical Killing and the Psychology of Genocide*. New York: Basic Books, 1986.

Lindbergh, Charles A. *The Wartime Journals of Charles A. Lindbergh*. New York: Harcourt Brace Jovanovich, 1970.

Lindemann, Albert S. *The Jew Accused: Three Anti-Semitic Affairs (Dreyfus, Beilis, Frank)*. New York: Cambridge University Press, 1991.

Lingens-Reiner, Ella. *Prisoners of Fear*. London: Gollancz, 1948.

Lipstadt, Deborah E. *Beyond Belief: The American Press and the Coming of the Holocaust, 1933–1945*. New York: The Free Press, 1986.

Lipstadt, Deborah E. *Denying the Holocaust: The Growing Assault on Truth and Memory*. A research project of The Vidal Sassoon International Center for the Study of Antisemitism of The Hebrew University of Jerusalem. New York: The Free Press, 1993.

Lochner, Louis P., ed. and trans. *The Goebbels Diaries 1942–1943*. Garden City, N.Y.: Doubleday, 1948.

Luell, Steven A., and Paul Marcus. *Psychoanalytic Reflections on the Holocaust: Selected Essays*. New York: Holocaust Awareness Institute Center for Judaic Studies, University of Denver, and Ktav, 1984.

Macdonald, Dwight. *Memoirs of a Revolutionist: Essays in Political Criticism*. New York: Farrar, Straus and Cudahy, 1957.

Marcus, Jacob R. *The Jew in the Medieval World*. Sinai Press, 1938. Reprinted, Westport, CT: Greenwood Press.

Marrus, Michael R. and Robert O. Paxton, *Vichy France and the Jews*. New York: Schocken Books, 1983. Originally published as *Vichy et les Juifs* by Editions Calmann-Levy.

Morgan, Michael L., ed. *The Jewish Thought of Emil Fackenheim: A Reader*. Detroit: Wayne State University Press, 1987.

Morley, John F. *Vatican Diplomacy and the Jews During the Holocaust, 1939–1943*. New York: Ktav, 1980.

Our Age. Volumes 1–7. New York: United Synagogue Commission on Jewish Education, 1959–1966.

Owings, Alison. *Frauen: German Women Recall the Third Reich*. New Brunswick, NJ: Rutgers University Press, 1993.

Perkins, Frances. *The Roosevelt I Knew*. New York: Viking Press, 1946.

Perry, Marvin, and Frederick M. Schweitzer, eds. *Jewish-Christian Encounters Over the Centuries: Symbiosis, Prejudice, Holocaust, Dialogue*. New York: Peter Lang, 1994.

Persico, Joseph E. *Nuremberg: Infamy on Trial*. New York: Viking Penguin, 1994.

Posner, Gerald L. *Hitler's Children: Sons and Daughters of Leaders of the Third Reich Talk About Their Fathers and Themselves*. New York: Random House, 1991.

Proudhon, Pierre-Joseph. *Caesar and Christianity*, 1883.

Ramras-Rauch, Gila, and Joseph Michman-Melkman, eds. *Facing the Holocaust: Israeli Fiction*. Philadelphia: Jewish Publication Society, 1985.

Rauschning, Hermann. *The Voice of Destruction*. New York: G. P. Putnam's Sons, 1940. By arrangement with Alliance Book Corp.

Read, Anthony and David Fisher. *Kristallnacht: The Nazi Night of Terror*. New York: Random House, 1989.

Reichel, Sabine. *What Did You Do in the War, Daddy?: Growing Up German*. New York: Hill and Wang, 1989.

Reinharz, Jehuda, ed. *The Letters and Papers of Chaim Weizmann*. Jerusalem: 1977. Reprinted, New York: Oxford University Press.

Reitlinger, Gerald. *The Final Solution*. New York: Yoseloff, 1968.

Ringelblum, Emmanuel. *Notes from the Warsaw Ghetto: The Journal of Emmanuel Ringelblum*. Edited and translated by Jacob Sloan. New York: McGraw-Hill, 1958.

Rittner, Carol and Sondra Myers, eds. *The Courage to Care: Rescuers of Jews During the Holocaust*. New York: New York University Press, 1986.

Roosevelt, Franklin D. *Our Sons Will Triumph*. New York: Thomas Y. Crowell, 1944.

Rosenberg, Alfred. *The World Struggle* (April, 1941).

Roth, Cecil, editor-in-chief. *The Standard Jewish Encyclopedia*. Garden City, NY: Doubleday & Co., 1959.

Rothchild, Sylvia, ed. *Voices from the Holocaust*. From the William E. Wener Oral History Library of the American Jewish Committee. New York: New American Library, 1981.

Ryan, Michael D., ed. *Human Responses to the Holocaust: Perpetrators and Victims, Bystanders and Resisters*. Papers of the 1979 Bernhard E. Olson Scholars Conference on "The Church Struggle and the Holocaust," sponsored by the National Conference of Christians and Jews. New York: Edwin Mellen Press, 1981.

Samuel, Maurice. *Blood Accusation*. New York: Knopf, 1966.

Shirer, William L. *The Rise and Fall of the Third Reich*. New York: Simon & Schuster, 1960.

Snyder, Louis L. *Louis L. Snyder's Historical Guide to World War II*. Westport, CT: Greenwood Press, 1982.

Speer, Albert. *Inside the Third Reich*. Translated from the German by Richard and Clara Winston. New York: Macmillan, 1970.

Stember, Charles Herbert. *Jews in the Mind of America*. New York: Basic Books, 1966.

Suhl, Yuri, ed. and trans. *They Fought Back*. New York: Schocken Books, 1975.

Trunk, Isaiah. *Judenrat: The Jewish Councils in Eastern Europe Under Nazi Occupation*. New York: Macmillan, 1972.

Twain, Mark. *Concerning the Jews*. Philadelphia: Running Press, 1985. Originally appeared in *Harper's*, 1898.

Van Paassen, Pierre. *A Pilgrim's Vow*. New York: Dial Press, 1956.

Vatican II. *The Documents of Vatican II*. New York: America Press, 1966.

von Lang, Jochen, ed. in collaboration with Claus Sibyn. *Eichmann Interrogated: Transcripts from the Archives of the Israeli Police*. Translated from the German by Ralph Manheim. New York: Farrar, Straus & Giroux, 1983.

Vrba, Rudolf and Alan Bestic. *I Cannot Forgive*. 1964.

Wasserstein, Bernard. *Britain and the Jews of Europe, 1939–1945*. London: Oxford University Press, 1979.

Watts, Franklin, and Nathan Ausubel, eds. *Voices of History*. New York: Gramercy Publishing Co., 1944.

Weiss, John. *Ideology of Death: Why the Holocaust Happened in Germany*. Chicago: Ivan R. Dee, 1996.

Wiesenthal, Simon. *Every Day Remembrance Day: A Chronicle of Jewish Martyrdom*. New York: Henry Holt & Co., 1987.

Wolffsohn, Michael. *Eternal Guilt? Forty Years of German-Jewish-Israeli Relations*. Translated by Douglas Bokovoy. New York: Columbia University Press, 1993.

Wyman, David S. *Paper Walls*. New York: Pantheon Books, 1968.

Wyman, David S. *The Abandonment of the Jews: America and the Holocaust, 1941–1945*. New York: Pantheon Books, 1984.

Zangwill, Israel. *Voice of Jerusalem*. 1921.

Ziemer, Gregor. *Education for Death*. New York: Oxford University Press, 1941.

Index

About the Author

Howard J. Langer is an author and freelance writer. His most recent book was *American Indian Quotations* (1996). Before turning to full-time writing, he was Publications Director of the Anti-Defamation League, where he wrote and edited materials on civil rights, Jewish history, and the Holocaust. Educated at Columbia University Graduate School of Journalism, he has worked for newspapers, magazines, and book publishers. Other published works include *The American Revolution, Who Put the Print on the Page?*, and *Directory of Speakers*. His recorded interviews with famous Americans are part of the Smithsonian/Folkways collection.